ST☉P
People
Pleasing

Chase Hill is a life coach and social interaction specialist, and has spent over a decade researching psychology, with a focus on mental attitude, emotional resilience, and assertiveness and boundary-setting in the modern world.

With a professional background in life coaching and a passion for helping others to unleash their true potential, Chase's writing is warm and refreshingly honest. His willingness to share personal stories from his own life, combined with his clear style and focused advice, makes it easy for readers to implement changes immediately.

Chase is an advocate for living the life you want to live, and makes sure to carve out the time for his own passions within his work. When he's not focusing on helping other people do the same, you might find him traveling the world, producing music, or hunting down his favourite records on vinyl.

He is the bestselling author of *How to Stop Overthinking*, a book which has hurtled to take Amazon's #1 Bestseller spot in both the US and the UK.

STOP People Pleasing
HOW TO START SAYING NO

CHASE HILL

RUPA

Published by
Rupa Publications India Pvt. Ltd 2025
7/16, Ansari Road, Daryaganj
New Delhi 110002

Sales centres:
Bengaluru Chennai
Hyderabad Jaipur Kathmandu
Kolkata Mumbai Prayagraj

Copyright © Chase Hill 2025

The views and opinions expressed in this book are the author's
own and the facts are as reported by him which have been
verified to the extent possible, and the publishers are not in
any way liable for the same.

All rights reserved.
No part of this publication may be reproduced, transmitted,
or stored in a retrieval system, in any form or by any means, electronic,
mechanical, photocopying, recording or otherwise, without the prior
permission of the publisher.

P-ISBN: 978-93-5702-892-9
E-ISBN: 978-93-5702-678-9

First impression 2025

10 9 8 7 6 5 4 3 2 1

The moral right of the author has been asserted.

Printed in India

This book is sold subject to the condition that it shall not, by way of
trade or otherwise, be lent, resold, hired out, or otherwise circulated,
without the publisher's prior consent, in any form of binding or
cover other than that in which it is published.

Contents

Introduction — 1

1. Detecting the Problem of People Pleasing — 5
2. Who Am I? An Exciting Self-Discovery Journey — 19
3. People Pleasing Mindset Hacking—Five Tiny and Powerful Habits — 34
4. How to Set Healthy Boundaries without Fear — 46
5. Start Saying No in Seconds without Feeling Guilty — 65
6. Dealing with People's Reactions — 77
7. How to Express Yourself and Build Genuine, Strong Friendships — 90
8. How to Stand Up for Yourself: 8 Assertiveness Techniques — 106
9. Troubleshooting Guide: What if Nothing Seems to Be Working? — 116
10. Taking Action to Stop People Pleasing in Two Weeks — 124

Conclusion — 132
References — 137

Introduction

The problem with people pleasing is that you're aware of it all unfolding, but you feel powerless to do anything about it. It is also obvious that what the other person is suggesting isn't going to make you happy. You want to say no, but you are frozen in fear of what their reaction might be or having to give a reason why.

So, you say yes, even if you don't want to. Unfortunately, this has happened to me a lot. But one event comes to my mind.

A few years ago, my friends decided to have a get-together to catch up and do something different for a change. At first, I honestly liked the idea. A break from routine is always a welcome change. My friends put forward ideas for activities, and I was powerless to voice my opinion. So afterward, when they decided to go camping and horseback riding, my enthusiasm started to dwindle.

I do like the outdoors, but I would have preferred going hiking in the mountains. I should have voiced my idea, but I didn't have the confidence and so I said yes. As a result, I was deeply upset during our adventure but continued smiling and telling everyone, "It's okay," "I'm fine," and, "Maybe next time."

But it wasn't okay. Even my horse sensed how terrified I was as I trotted off in the opposite direction from my friends. "At least my friends are happy," I told myself. But deep down, I knew that something big had to change.

You may not have been riding a horse or had a mouth full of midges when your moment of realization hit, but we have all had a situation when we understood that a drastic change had to be made. That you simply can't go on saying yes to everyone and everything while you suffer the consequences.

People pleasing seems harmless. I only wanted to be a good friend and keep the crowd happy. But this disorder can have some very detrimental impacts on your life. The inability to say no essentially leads us to do things we don't want to, meaning we rarely find the time for ourselves, and eventually, we forget what we actually love doing.

It's an exhausting and overwhelming feeling to always have to be the peacekeeper and keep everyone happy. Each situation requires a different strategy and different skills. You might have to be the sympathizer, listening and agreeing to a friend's problems, or perhaps the friend who has to go shopping or to a certain restaurant when you would rather not. The longer the situation goes on, the further away from your true self you become until you are completely lost and unaware of who you are.

The fear of saying no can even prevent you from taking part in the things you think you may enjoy. You want to go to the family reunion, but what if there is a situation you don't like and aren't able to say no? Slowly, you retreat back into your own shell and prefer a life of solitude because it is just safer that way.

People pleasing seeps into every part of your life: your job, your relationships, your family, and your friends. It is a painful suffering that eats away at your motivation, drains your energy, and stops you from achieving your goals.

Introduction

I was in the same situation, and it was spiraling out of control. I was terrified of upsetting my girlfriend, and she ended up leaving me because she became so frustrated at my inability to defend my wishes and beliefs. My career in finance was dull and monotonous. There were plenty of opportunities for advancement, but nobody noticed me over others in the office who could speak their mind without fear of repercussions.

I spent the majority of my 20s people pleasing. I wanted to be the nice guy and to make sure everyone was getting what they wanted from life. I was desperate to be a good boyfriend, son, colleague, and friend. My grandmother died, and I knew I was never going to be able to grant her wish for great-grandchildren. This was the final straw to an already emotional and impossible situation.

I decided that I would have to fight my way out of my people pleasing disorder, one small win at a time. I studied and learned to appreciate how specific behaviors and personalities led to people pleasing. With small, simple steps, I was able to turn my life around and see things in a new, fresh, and positive light. I rediscovered inspiration, which led to new goals. I learned how to be happy.

It wasn't just my studies that enabled me to change my life. I went through ups and downs the following year and learned a lot from the choices I could have made differently, but the results were truly amazing. I am grateful for my failed relationship and my experience in finance—without it, I may not have been so determined to set my own boundaries and stop people pleasing.

I am going to show you how you don't need to give up your desire to help people—after all, it's a wonderful personality trait to have. But I will also show you how to keep this under control so that you don't forget your own happiness or place the needs of others ahead of your own.

This is what we are going to do in this book. Together, we will create an action plan that will allow you to achieve a different mindset, one that will take you from a place of emptiness to one filled with self-appreciation and enjoyment for life.

This book is broken down into stages that follow the logical path of learning how to stop people pleasing. We will learn how to: set boundaries, handle the fear of other people's reactions, and express ideas and feelings with assertion and without the fear of offending others. You will become the master of social situations, the master of your relationships, and the master of your career.

We are going to work through a number of techniques and tools that will help you to start making a difference in your life. Additionally, I have prepared a 14 Day Action Plan for those who need guidance and instant, noticeable improvements. You can find it at the end of the book.

But the first step is to understand exactly what people pleasing is, how it is rooted inside you, and how it has become a part of who you are. So, if you are ready to start saying no, then sit back, enjoy the experience, and keep reading.

1
Detecting the Problem of People Pleasing

A people pleaser is someone who cares a lot about what people think of them. They lack assertion and constantly seek the approval of others. The extent of people pleasing can vary greatly. For example, it could happen only with a certain group of people, like colleagues or managers.

Children have been known to be complete teacher-pleasers in the school environment but refuse to do anything a parent asks them. This is far from a disorder or a sign that it will continue into adult life, but it does go to show that wanting to make others happy isn't restricted to age. As we go through our teenage years, we battle with the need to be liked by friends and the desire to be our own person.

Mild to serious cases can have a significant impact on one's life. These people may struggle with finding their own happiness, either because they don't know what it looks like, or because they put the happiness of others before their own.

For those who have a people pleasing disorder, the problem consumes their entire life. From morning to evening. They fear disrupting the peace by voicing their opinions. Even when asked, they will offer answers that others want to hear rather than their honest views. They will worry about how colleagues, family members, friends, and even strangers view them.

And then there is the big one—they fear saying the word no, which leads to quick yes responses. The degree of fear is also variable, but when the idea of saying no makes you feel sick to your stomach, your life is no longer your own. People may have attempted to say no in the past, and the guilt that comes forth due to them having to upset someone is so overwhelming that they are unwilling to decline in future situations.

A simple example is choosing clothes in the morning. Rarely will people pleasers put on something that makes them feel confident and comfortable. Instead, they will wear something that others will approve of. Even the decision of what clothes to buy will be based on whether others will like the clothes, rather than what clothes they like.

What makes people pleasing hard to accept as a problem is that we are taught that being nice and thinking about other people's feelings are important. The truth is, it is important, and wanting to please people is a lovely characteristic to have, but when you start to bend over backwards to such an extent that it impacts your own emotions, then it becomes a harmful problem.

People Pleasing and the Draining Effects

For the people pleaser, life itself is just exhausting. From eating Chinese when you wanted Italian, to moving cities because your partner wanted to, and everything in between, each situation that forces you to say yes can tap away a little bit of your happiness.

Detecting the Problem of People Pleasing

All of your efforts are devoted to the well-being of others. You want to help them and fix their problems. Some people don't realize the toll this takes on their life. Every action you carry out for someone else takes away some of your time and energy. Again, this isn't a bad thing as long as there is a balance.

But when all of your efforts are turned toward making other people happy, you end up feeling exhausted. Particularly when the people in your life keep coming back with more problems for you to deal with and additional issues that you don't really want to be involved in.

You will feel tired and drained if you are consistently trying hard to help others. It's difficult to make an imperfect world perfect. People pleasing can lead to frustration and anger as you may feel as though you have too many responsibilities and that nobody is there to support you.

The need to please people is part of our nature, and those with a people pleasing disorder will not be able to just stop. It is more likely that, despite being tired and angry, you will still try to make others happy. This is when the problem becomes harmful.

Why People Pleasing is Harmful

On the one hand, you may feel so suffocated by the problem that you find yourself with additional medical symptoms. In my situation, I felt my physical health decline and the problem become more serious.

The pressure to please, saying yes to everything, and the focus on other people's feelings rather than my own led me into depression. It was very difficult for me to find motivation in life. I would dread going to work and felt relieved when I returned home to be alone. I rarely met with my friends because it was just easier that way.

I did no exercise. I felt a few pounds pile on and a few aches and pains that a man of my age shouldn't yet experience. My sleep patterns were out of balance and this added to my lack of energy.

According to a study published in the *Natural Neuroscience* journal, people pleasing can alter the way you behave and diminish your sense of integrity. You start to tell white lies in order to provide the desired answer in a conversation. These white lies are harmless at first, but it then becomes easier to tell bigger lies, ones that can be more harmful. Before you know it, you are a completely different person who is caught up in a web of lies that goes against who you actually are.

People pleasing is also a sign of poor self-awareness. We are so desperate to do things that, to gain a sense of worth, we often say yes to something we don't want to do so that we don't look bad in front of those we're trying to please. Whether that is drinking too much, experimenting with illegal drugs, or driving too fast, we put ourselves in physical danger.

How People Pleasing Can Be Exhausting for Those Who Love Us

When I attended my university, I had a friend who was a complete people pleaser. At this point, I still felt I was a good person trying to make others happy, so I wasn't aware that some of his traits were reflected in myself.

During the four years we studied together, he would regularly come around to my parent's house for dinner. The first night we had pasta and tomato sauce. When my mom asked if he liked it, he replied that it was absolutely delicious and ate the entire bowl. Mom has never been a great cook, so this compliment was enough for her to make it every time Ryan came around for dinner.

Toward the end of our studies, he and I went to a restaurant one night and, while ordering, he told the waiter that he didn't like tomatoes. Seeing my surprised face, he turned almost the same color as the sauce he had been eating at my house for years. That first night he couldn't bring himself to upset my mom, and then after a few dinners it had become impossible for him to confess his dislike for tomatoes.

People pleasing is also difficult for the people who love us and see that we have a problem. It is hard to watch a person suffer because they can't put their own feelings first. Trying to make that person happy, while understanding the difficulties they have expressing their real feelings, can be exhausting. It takes a lot of effort and sometimes may even push loved ones away.

This is certainly no reason for you to feel guiltier than you already do. But when you learn how to start saying no, you will be able to look forward to your loved ones feeling a little more relieved that life is going the way you want it to.

Deep Roots of People Pleasing

The important question that I asked myself, and you probably have too, is how this need to please and the inability to say no arises. It wasn't something that just happened, like a cold or an illness. I felt that I had always been a good person, but when did this get out of control?

For me to be able to overcome the problem, I needed to get to the root cause to understand why I was the way I was.

If you have ever spent time with a psychologist, you may have noticed the tendency to look into childhood and consider the relationship with the parents. It was Freud who suggested that mental health problems were caused by unconscious emotional problems experienced in childhood.

But the problem with this way of thinking is that it tends to lead to the word "blame" and the belief that all issues we experience in our adult lives are caused by our parents' mistakes.

When you look at the bigger picture, parenthood is incredibly hard to perfect. Parents can show too much love and be smothering, they can be too strict, or they may not set strong enough boundaries. They may be too absent and not show enough love. In certain cases, parents are too narcissistic and can put their own needs above those of their children's.

Getting the right combination of parenting skills is a very tricky balance. Plus, parents are still only human, and they will have their own problems to try and get through.

When I look back at my childhood, nothing sticks out. My parents are still together, and they always showed each other, and myself, love and respect. It all felt quite normal. But then this is the point—it is our subconscious that has absorbed the behavior of our parents' and manifested into people pleasing.

As we move through the process of getting to the root of people pleasing, I don't want you to take anything we say or what you feel about your parents to heart. It isn't a blame game, and the chances are that, even if they are indeed the root of the problem, there was no intention on their behalf.

How the Relationship with Our Parents Impacts Our Need to Please

There are a few possible links between childhood relationships and people pleasing in adulthood. One of the principal causes of our behavior is the lack of parental attunement. Attunement is the way we form our relationships, and how we adapt ourselves to ensure it is a harmonious relationship.

When parents are not around, children miss the opportunity to be able to connect with their parents on a deeper level. There isn't a chance for emotions to be explored and expressed. Parents are either not present physically as they have to work away or for long hours, or they are not present emotionally because they are too caught up in their own lives.

Again, this is not necessarily the parent's fault. A mother or father may work hard so that the family has a good income and be able to enjoy the finer things in life. On the other hand, they also may be struggling with mental illnesses. This can lead to parents not being able to cope with a child's feelings or even misinterpreting a child's feelings because they are too consumed by their own emotions.

The result of this is that the child takes on the role of caregiver, essentially stepping into the shoes of the parent. In their role as protector, the child is still able to feel a connection with their parents. In this situation, the worrying for others begins at a young age.

Another parental behavior that can trigger people pleasing is when one or both of the parents are emotionally unstable. They tend to blow hot and cold, being adorably loving one moment and angry or aggressive the next. If a young child has grown up with this, they may see it as normal and not question the happiness of their childhood. As adults, we look back to see predominately good memories, either because we have blocked out the bad, or we assumed it was normal. Bear in mind that we are not talking about physical abuse here.

When a parent is emotionally unstable, a young child learns very early on how to gauge a person's mood and emotions. They will adapt their own behaviors to match the needs of their parents. They go out of their way to keep the peace and try to make their parents proud. The child's good behavior stems from the need to keep people happy, rather than because it's the right thing to do.

As I was studying psychology, I could certainly see the logic behind these theories. However, I didn't feel like this was relevant in my situation. Granted, my parents and I still fought and had our ups and downs but nothing out of the ordinary. If you feel the same about your childhood, there is an alternative to the lack of connection.

Detecting the Problem of People Pleasing

I discovered that my people pleasing came about from an extreme fear of disappointing others. My mom was the fusser in the family. She showed me what it was like to look after people. It is possible that she has a hint of people pleasing in her. My father was strong. He ran his own business, and he has high standards and a strong work ethic. I looked up to both of my parents.

Growing up, we go through certain stages in regard to the relationship we have with our parents. We start loving them and depending on them. As teenagers, we rebel and test the limits of that love. Part of becoming an adult is learning that our parents are not perfect, forgiving them for their mistakes. Somewhere between sixteen and seventeen years old, I started to really appreciate how lucky I was. I respected the dynamics of my family, and after everything that my parents had done for me, I became determined not to disappoint them.

I finished university with a better degree than any of us had expected, and my parents were elated. Seeing them so proud, talking to their friends about me, felt amazing. And it's a feeling I wanted to keep experiencing.

So, when I got my first job, once again, my parents were ecstatic. From here, I couldn't do anything wrong to mess this up because I couldn't afford to disappoint them. The chain of people pleasing grew. I couldn't disappoint my boss because I couldn't risk losing my job. I couldn't put my ideas forward because my boss might be displeased. Then this behavior started appearing in other areas of my life. I had to get a girlfriend that my parents liked. I couldn't go traveling for six months because I worried about my parents.

And so, though I didn't have a bad childhood, I had a personality that was prone to people pleasing in order not to disappoint. What began as an innocent hope of pleasing my parents turned into a disorder that would take control of my entire life.

Take some time to discover the root cause of your reason for people pleasing, not because you need to find someone to blame or to hold responsible, but because it will provide you with better insight into your inner world. See it as the pre-healing.

Another tool you might want to use is a self-awareness test. Asking yourself some simple questions will show you when the act of being nice and caring about others has progressed into a people pleasing problem.

♦

Awareness Test: Discover the Depth of Your People Pleasing Problem

People pleasing is not just about the inability to say no. While working with psychologists and clinical social workers, I put together a list of ten other signs that indicate people pleasing characteristics aside from not being able to speak up for your emotions and desires.

1. Do you constantly apologize?

This could be because you feel like you are always in the wrong or you are under the impression that others blame you. Taking responsibility for your actions is very noble but only when it is called for.

2. Do you feel responsible for the emotions of others?

You will notice other people's happiness or sadness will depend on you. Remember, you do have the ability to make someone happy or sad, but they also have the choice to control how they feel.

3. Do you agree with people, regardless of your opinions?

Sometimes, the best solution for social occasions is to agree so as not to spark a great debate. That being said, when you are agreeing with people for the sake of being liked, you are changing a part of who you really are.

4. Does it upset you when someone shows anger toward you?

The sheer thought of someone being angry because of something you did may also be enough to change part of your true self. Even if you haven't done anything wrong, people pleasers find this a very nerve-racking experience.

5. Do you feel pressured to do things you don't want to do?

I have touched on this before, and it could be something trivial like where to go shopping or something far more significant like the location of your new home. When you agree to do things that you don't want to do, you are effectively giving the control of your life to someone else.

6. Do you see yourself mirroring the behavior of others?

It is rare that someone acts the same way with their mother-in-law as they do with their friends; humans are good at adapting their behavior to various social situations. The issue becomes clear when you can't say no to the last drink, or you take unnecessary risks to fit in with the people around you.

7. Do you go out of your way to avoid arguments?

Some people seem to thrive on conflict and heated discussions. People pleasers will do the opposite because they find it impossible to defend their side of the argument. It's like a one-sided battle from the get-go.

8. Are kind words and praise essential for your happiness?

Everybody loves a compliment and, to an extent, needs one every now and then. A people pleaser struggles to feel any form of self-worth. When we receive any form of praise, it reinforces the idea that people think positively about us, something that is necessary as we find it difficult to do this ourselves.

9. Do you hide your hurt feelings?

That time when someone says, "Sorry, did I offend you?" and you laugh it off with a no when really even a small comment or action has deeply upset you.

When you are unable to let others know if something embarrasses you, enrages you, or irritates you, you will find that your relationships do not have a genuine connection.

10. Do you struggle to find free time?

A classic sign of people pleasing dominating your life is when you can't seem to find any time for yourself. The need to say yes to everybody means your days, weeks, and months become occupied with fulfilling the needs of others.

How strongly you agree with each of these questions will provide insight into the extent of your people pleasing disorder. Some will agree with most of them and perhaps some more than others. There are people who can relate so strongly with the questions they feel they have been written just for them.

Be careful not to start taking too many online self-awareness tests. Some of the questions focus on people's perceptions of you rather than how you view yourself.

Our focus is to determine what you feel about yourself as we have spent enough time concerning ourselves with the views of others.

◆

Why It's Important to Overcome People Pleasing

For an outsider, the problem may seem like you are too busy, you are a bit tired, you have a rather neutral personality, or you are never one to rock the boat. Those who are suffering from people pleasing are not just tired, they are emotionally and physically exhausted. They have taken away so much of who they really are to make sure they are accepted that they feel like an empty shell or even a chameleon, constantly trying to switch between the personalities they have created to keep others happy.

Nobody should have to go through life feeling as if they have to be quiet or be the person in the room whose opinions are never heard. Nobody should have to feel like they have to hide their emotions or tiptoe around. If you can relate to feeling like a pinball being pinged around the machine all the time, it's time to start making changes.

If you are reading this book, you are probably aware of that you have an issue with people pleasing. Hopefully, now you are able to appreciate the extent of your problem so that we can move forward and start creating a solution. Now that we have identified the issue, it's time to peel back the layers to discover who we really are. Overcoming people pleasing for good requires us first to look at who we truly are on the inside. If you can't remember what you love and what you hate, you need to get to the bottom of these questions. When we are able to see our needs and passions, we can set the foundations for a significant, positive change.

2

Who Am I? An Exciting Self-Discovery Journey

Surprisingly, you may need to come to terms with identifying yourself as a people pleaser. When I did, I knew that if I wanted to make a change in my life, I would have to first learn who I was. But this wasn't necessarily about who I was on the surface. I needed to go deeper until I was almost, metaphorically speaking, back to the skeleton. We have become so lost in doing what is good for others, and as a result, we have no idea where to begin with what is good for us.

If you were to ask me at the beginning of my journey who I was, the answer would have been rather reserved. Even I felt bored listening to my description, and I didn't want to put that on anyone else. I was a man in my late 20s, working in finance. I was single and lived alone. Full stop. I could have said I liked watching TV and walking, but none of this genuinely defined me, and it was certainly no wonder I was single.

I needed to get past what was on the surface and get down to the nitty-gritty—the meaningful stuff. This was a challenge in itself because as you can imagine by now, I wasn't very good at expressing my feelings and with the months that I had been through, I didn't even know how—if I could even define how—I was feeling to myself.

Be Aware of Defense Mechanisms

Defense mechanisms are another concept from Freud, and this particular theory is still considered significant today. A defense mechanism is the way our subconscious employs strategies to protect itself from nervous and anxious thoughts and emotions. For us, this is how we defend our actions, and tell ourselves that it's okay to be a people pleaser because we are simply putting others first.

There are eight major defense mechanisms, but we are going to focus on those that are specific to pleasing others.

- **Denial:** We refuse to acknowledge the actions or emotions that have led to the anxiety we feel.
- **Repression:** We block out our experiences, preventing them from entering our consciousness.
- **Rationalization:** We justify why we are the way we are or why we do things. It's typical when we tell ourselves that they needed the promotion more than we did.
- **Reaction Formation:** We tend to act in contrary to our true feelings or say the opposite to what we want to say. We say yes when we want to say no.

> *"Defenses keep us stuck in one unhappy place.*
> *It takes truth and courage to abandon them,*
> *but once we do, we discover a world of*
> *freedom and wonderful possibilities."*
>
> —Dorothy Rowe, psychologist

For us to get to the bottom of who we really are, it is necessary to watch out for these defense mechanisms and not allow ourselves to be influenced. Now that you are aware of them, there are certain ways that you can respond to them. For example, you could try to separate your emotions with the situation that caused them and take some time to process your feelings and actually feel them.

Talking to yourself in the mirror may sound foolish, but you can have a conversation with your defense mechanisms. Play the role of yourself and then listen to why they are trying to protect you. Learn how these reactions are keeping you in the situation you are in rather than allowing you to move forward.

The Start of Your Self-Discovery

You can begin by playing a little game. You want to define yourself in terms of your emotions and your physical self. As soon as you begin, you will notice that you can only focus on the negative qualities, for instance, "My eyes are too small," "I am pale," "I don't like to try new foods," etc. If this is the case, you must immediately stop this little experiment. Tear up the paper, and we need to start again.

The new game for self-discovery, for those who focused on negatives, has stricter rules. For every negative thing you can find about yourself, you absolutely have to list a positive observation along with it. The game now goes along the lines of: "My eyes are too small, but they have a beautiful, piercing blue color," or "I am a little pale, but..."

When you start a mission, like understanding who you are, it can be incredibly overwhelming. It's an emotional rollercoaster, and you have waves of feeling great and waves of feeling awful. It is also an activity that cannot be done with any sense of pressure or hurry. I began with lots of "Uhmm," "Well," and "Maybe." Here is where you may notice your defense mechanisms kicking in. But after about an hour of being committed to answering this profound question, you will get into a flow.

This game is similar to opening Pandora's box, and things will just pour out. It can be amazing, but it will also be a learning experience that is incomparable to any online course or degree. It is very likely that you will go through something similar again, and either way, this will be an amazing experience. Nevertheless, be careful not to fall into the same trap as many do with focusing on the negatives.

The longer your lists grow, the more you will understand that you have good things about yourself and in your life. Unfortunately, as people pleasers, it is more likely that we will focus on the negatives. However, the wave of negativity often brings about a sense of urgency that we must fix everything immediately.

You will find that as you come to the end of your list, you will have a few things of what you might call the "fix me list." We feel that these are things we would like to change if we want to change our lives. When you start to feel the same way about all of your flaws, you end up with a list of things to try, fix, or do in a period of time that is not realistic. Unfortunately, this leads to further disappointment, and so the cycle continues.

When you don't achieve something on your list the very next day, you feed the cycle of negativity and disappointment. While on the path to discovering who you are, you will appreciate that having a separate list of things you want to improve is a good way to remove the pressure of fixing everything now. Solutions will come quickly, but not overnight.

Finally, you will have three lists. The list of things you like, one that needs some changes in mentality and another that will take more time to explore new things.

I am going to provide you with some of the things that were on my initial list, but please remember that this has to be your personal list. I recommend you take inspiration from my experiences and use them to explore who you are.

List 1: What I liked about myself

The physical aspects that should be used as a way to gain confidence in social surroundings. For example, I was no supermodel, but I wasn't ugly either. On that note, nobody is with regards to their looks.

I learned that I needed to concentrate on this list when I was out with friends or in the office. Confidence was an essential part of my discovery, and it will be for yours as well. Make sure your list has a number of factors that make you feel proud of who you are.

List 2: What I needed to change about myself right away

When I looked at my mentality, I discovered a lot of my problems came down to my lack of confidence. I felt timid when in groups because I didn't have faith in my own valuable opinions.

I watched BBC, CBN, Fox, etc. I had a good general knowledge of the world, and with this knowledge, I could form solid opinions. It was my confidence that prevented me to voice them because I was afraid of someone disagreeing with me.

List 3: What I discovered about myself that would require more time

These were the things that I felt if I put too much pressure on myself, the results would be counterproductive. Wanting to lose the excess weight in a month is setting yourself up for failure. My discovery taught me how much I wanted to lose weight, and while this would make me happy, it was going to take a long-term plan in order to succeed.

Similarly, I hated my car. I didn't feel like it was a suitable car for someone in the finance industry. Would you believe that I used to park my little Fiesta down the road instead of in the staff parking lot so that people wouldn't judge me on my car? When you step out of the people pleasing condition, you can clearly see that driving a Fiesta or a Ferrari had no relation to the ability to do my job. Nevertheless, my heart desired a new car, and so it went on my third list.

My most significant discovery was that I was a nice man. I tried to do good. I wanted to see other people happy as this made me happy. If I spent the last $50 on a new blender for my mom and saw her eyes light up as she went on about what she was going to make me, this was enough to make me feel like I had made her life a little better.

I also learned that if I had spent that $50 on my mom, instead of buying, for example, the two new tires my little Fiesta needed, then I was harming myself and my mom. I could get into trouble with the law or even have an accident. My dad would highlight the problem of my tires, and this would cause my mom to worry. So, the act of making my mom happy had greater consequences on me and the happiness of my family.

Getting a Complete Picture of Who You Are

A complete picture of who you are is like taking a step out of your skin and looking at the bigger picture. Your journey to self-discovery started by taking a close look at the physical and emotional qualities you liked and disliked about yourself, and we worked on defining our goals so we could create some direction. Now we will discover more about our passions, analyze our relationships, and find the best ways to deal with our emotions as they surface.

It is such a profound question that it is impossible to answer this in the space of an hour or two. I noticed that after my first stage of self-discovery, more and more came to mind in different scenarios.

I went for a walk one afternoon and started to appreciate the lush green of the grass and the beauty that was all around me. When you turn on the news and see all the negativity in the world, it is easy to lose track of all the simple yet amazing things. During this walk, I discovered I was interested in the planet and ways we could look after it better. I realized the persistent chirping of birds was actually quite irritating for me. I also recognized that if I had been walking with someone else who happened to love the sound, I would have agreed.

If you are reading this book, it is because you realize you need a change, and this change will not take very long. That being said, discovering who you are cannot be rushed. If you hurry through this process, you are likely to arrive at the answer you think you want rather than the truth.

Once you have figured out who you really are, you can then go on to a few more exercises that will give you a clearer overall image of yourself. Let's look at four additional steps that will enable you to appreciate the real you.

Discover what you are good at and what you are not

As a people pleaser, you will often find yourself doing things that you are not good at because you don't want to upset the plans of others. I would dread the Sunday morning friendly football match or even when someone suggested 'watching the game.' Society wrongly assumes that all men like football, whereas it actually just bored me. The cost of following the crowd meant we never went skiing, something I was actually quite comfortable doing.

- Look back over your past and remember some of the things you used to do when you were younger.
- In your past, what were you doing when you were at your happiest?
- Look at your soft skills, your personal attributes; are you a good listener, do you have a good sense of humor, can you focus well?

- Look at your hard skills, those that you have learned over time; can you dance, play an instrument, are you good with computers?
- Try something new, even if it's just once a week, and if you don't like it straight away, don't give up.

There may be hobbies that you have wanted to start, and it turns out that you aren't very good at them. You may be inspired by a TV program to do something you had never thought of but find you are great at it.

If you take away the things that your friends, family, and colleagues encourage you to do, you are able to clear a path to understanding what you are good at.

Discover what you are passionate about

Your passions may be closely linked to what you are good at, but that isn't necessarily the case. Look at things that excite you and motivate you. These are the things that are going to make your life happy and fruitful. Remember that being passionate about helping people is a way of deflecting the problem. If helping in a soup kitchen makes you happy, then this can be considered a passion. But when the passion becomes an obligation, you are only feeding the disorder.

A passion for your work is crucial. I couldn't find any motivation in my financial career. I know my dad saw it as a huge achievement, but it wasn't something that got me excited. One of the greatest changes I made was in my career. My profession as a life coach sparked a fire inside me that pushes me to be a better person. Like the example of the soup kitchen, I am still able to help people, but I do it in my own way without the pressure of feeling like I have to.

Get some feedback from those closest to you

This is difficult for us and it involves opening up. Asking how others feel about us pulls the focus onto ourselves, and this is not normal. Sometimes it is hard to hear the feedback, or in the case of positive things, we find it hard to believe.

It is a good way to discover more about you because your loved ones might be able to offer insight into things you hadn't considered. Don't over-analyze the feedback but do take things from it because it can help you to find out more about yourself from a different point of view, often more optimistic than your own.

Evaluate your relationships

You need to understand if the people in your life are helping your problem or causing it. Essentially, it is you who can't say no, but unfortunately, there will be people in the world who take advantage of this and others who just assume it is part of your personality.

As we adapt our behavior in order to make others happy, we are chipping away a part of who we really are. When we can either remove these people, distance ourselves, or at least appreciate the control they have over us (whether conscious or unconscious), we will be able to better understand who we really are.

Learning to Cope with Your Emotions

Before your journey to self-discovery begins, it is also sensible to learn some tips on how to cope with your emotions. Your journey is at the initial stages, and while some of the education relates to learning about who you are now, there is another side that requires constant practice. And that is what to do when certain emotions creep up.

When a people pleaser is in a difficult situation, they will push their emotions to one side to deal with those of others. Some people will leave these emotions buried within them, and at some point, they will resurface. Normally much more powerful than they were in the beginning, whether that is a day later, a week, or longer.

Part of our journey is to learn how to cope with these emotions as they arise, rather than having to suffer the consequences at a later date. I have found that, to unblock the buildup of emotions, you need to find a way to release them.

I like to discuss four key methods to finding an outlet for emotions with my clients. Let's look at each one with some ideas on how to use every method.

Finding a physical outlet

Quite often, you will feel so much better by doing some form of physical exercise. The additional oxygen pumping around your body reduces stress, improves your concentration, and will improve your sleep.

I am a huge fan of the Wii. Before you laugh, go with me on this. The gym takes effort, time, and money. Quite often, just 10-15 minutes of some physical exercise on the Wii can brighten your mood. There is such a range of activities from boxing to yoga, and you can also enjoy some games that get you moving. Never in my life would I have skateboarded in the street, but I discovered a new passion when I played on this video console.

Even cleaning is a good way to physically release some stress. A really good scrub of the kitchen tiles lets out a bit of the pent-up aggression, and you will be happier with a cleaner kitchen.

Other physical releases include going for a walk or squeezing a stress ball. You could tap into your creative side and make your own stress balls with rice and a balloon.

Also, don't be scared to cry. Put on those songs that allow you to feel your emotions and cry. Imagine each tear as a part of that emotion being set free.

Find a creative way to release your emotions

Keeping a journal is a marvelous activity. Not only does it allow you to express your emotions, but you also don't have to worry about the repercussions of somebody else's feelings. Over time, you are able to look back on your emotions, understand their triggers, and see if there are any patterns.

Another creative activity is to start a scrapbook. I found that this helped me to focus on some of the more positive things I was experiencing. My scrapbook was a journey of my progress, and it helped me to appreciate some of my achievements, the places I had visited, and the new things I had tried.

Other options may involve painting, drawing, and coloring. There are some lovely adult coloring books on the market, and while you may think you are only distracting yourself, your subconscious is able to process emotions.

Some people even find that playing a musical instrument is a good outlet.

Focus on relaxing your body and mind

Deep breathing has a similar effect to exercise with regards to increasing the oxygen levels in your body. At the same time, it gives your mind time off from the stresses in life and a chance to focus on you.

Meditation and mindfulness both require a little practice, but the scientific benefits are now being proven. Specifically for us people pleasers, it will allow you to improve your self-awareness, manage anxiety, and reduce stress.

Treat yourself

Time alone to do what I want always seems to lift a weight off my shoulders. For example, taking a shower. It's one thing to have a shower in order to get ready for work, but it's another thing to put music on, shave, and have a shower that lasts as long as your hot water. Treat yourself to a bath, regardless of your gender. A warm bath without the pressure of time is like soaking your emotions away.

What Happens When Emotions Are Just Too Strong to Process?

There will have been and will continue to be moments when you just can't cope with the emotions because they are too strong. Whether you are feeling sadness, anger, frustration, or nerves, you won't be able to work through them if they are too fresh and too powerful. In this case, you need to focus on some actions that will immediately work to reduce the rawness of your emotions.

In the first place, you should go to your safe place. Sometimes this is an experience or memory that fills you with joy and takes away the initial pain of your emotions. It could also be a physical location, perhaps your bedroom, your balcony, or your local park. If you combine this with some deep breathing, you should feel the effects within a short time. If not, here are some other ideas:

- **Watch a TV series.** Some choose a movie, and this is a good idea but as a series is shorter, it will often capture your attention faster.
- **Take advantage of social media.** Lots of social media platforms have funny videos or titbits of information that can draw in your attention.
- **Turn to your passion.** Stop whatever it is that is causing your emotions to overheat and replace it with something that you love.
- **Play a game.** There are plenty of apps that have brain games, logic games, or games to test your coordination.

Playing doesn't have to take up a lot of time, but they will serve as a distraction.

If you try to start saying no to people when you haven't discovered who you truly are, you will end up with a mixed basket of apples and oranges. You might know that you want to change, and you will have created a plan to start the action, but you won't have provided yourself with all of the necessary tools that will assist you along the way.

Asking the question, "Who am I?" and following the steps to gain a deep understanding of who you are is the best way to lay the foundations to change your behavior so that you can focus on the things that will enhance your life.

3

People Pleasing Mindset Hacking — Five Tiny and Powerful Habits

When people look at their situation, it can seem like a never-ending battle. We have gotten to the root cause of our people pleasing, and we have dedicated some time to self-discovery and identifying what we want to achieve in order to be happy. But it still seems like there is a long way to go. To an extent this is true, but we are still only talking about less than a year now. The process shouldn't be an overnight miracle as you need time to learn about yourself and gain the confidence to say no in the right way.

One thing that I found helped tremendously in the early stages of transforming my life was to change five very small things that I was doing. These five things didn't depend on anybody else except me, and they allowed me to see almost instant results. Because they were things I could do, I found I wasn't asking too much too soon.

In my mind, I knew it would be the first small steps that would lead to the bigger changes I needed to see. Many of my clients have felt that practicing these five habits helped them gain momentum and then, seeing the positive effects, motivated them to keep going. Let's look at these five steps in detail.

Step 1. Being Aware of Unhealthy People Pleasing

As time goes by, people pleasing becomes such a strong part of our personality that it is hard to identify. It's a little bit like people who constantly swear, but they don't realize it. The difference is, because many people don't like a lot of foul language, it's easier for others to confront them on their bad habit.

People pleasing isn't the same, mainly because those around you benefit from your personality in this way. You are making their life better, easier, and happier, so even if they subconsciously know it is wrong, they generally aren't going to highlight your people pleasing behavior.

So, it is down to you to identify situations where you tend to people please. We have already been over the key characteristics of people pleasing, so now we will look closely at how we can be aware that we are about to say yes to something we don't want.

Ask yourself what you are feeling: The moment somebody makes a suggestion, you have a split-second emotion. It could be nervousness, sadness, dread, fear, panic, anger, etc. You can't just skip over the emotion, so put your finger on it and call it what it is.

Ask yourself what you want: This isn't just a yes or no answer. Maybe you do want to do what the person is suggesting, maybe you don't. Or perhaps there are some parts that sound good, but you would rather do it in a different way.

Ask yourself what you need: The obvious answer is that you need to please others, but if you get past this fact, you may realize you need an hour at the gym, or you need a long soak in the bath.

Ask yourself what you are scared of: A large part of our need to say yes is because we are scared of the consequences and how the other person will react. Maybe you are scared that if you say yes, you will find yourself in another situation where you are obliged to say yes again.

Saying no doesn't make you a bad person. Today I still say yes to a lot of things, but before I do, I need to take a little time to assess the situation and decide if I am saying yes because I feel I have to or because I want to. The idea is not to become a person who never helps or is selfish with their needs. We want to find a balance.

Although you may not be able to say no straight away, being aware of a people pleasing situation will make it easier for you to learn what to do. If you ask yourself the four questions mentioned above, you will have a clearer understanding of whether or not you want to do something and the reasons behind your decision.

Step 2. Learn to Be Thankful

Whenever a people pleaser receives a compliment, two things usually happen. The shock takes us by surprise and then our defense mechanisms start to kick in, such as denial. It is almost impossible for us to just say thank you.

More often than not, we then try to justify the compliment. Classic examples I have heard involve when you mention how nice someone's clothes are, and they respond that they are hopeless with fashion and their sister picked it out, or that the outfit was a present. When someone tells you how delicious your dinner was, and you reply by saying it was a lucky evening, or a super simple recipe.

These situations may not appear to be too damaging, but now look at these: when your wife or husband comments that you have done a great job decorating, and you attack them because you feel like they are patronizing your efforts. Not only have you hurt their feelings, but you may have also started an argument. Worse yet, they will be reluctant to pay you more flattering remarks in the future.

I wanted to break the habit of saying thank you and then continue the sentence with some form of explanation, and I felt like retraining the brain was necessary. So, I banned myself from saying the words "thank you" because this triggered me to keep talking. Instead, I learned how to reply to a compliment using other words:

- I really value your opinion
- I really appreciate what you did/said
- Your kind words made my day
- I'm really grateful
- I owe you one
- Cheers

Now, when someone says, "I like your haircut," I can say, "Cheers, I appreciate that,"—full stop! In the past, I would have passed the credit to my girlfriend. This habit is an excellent way to accept positive attention and not deflect it to others.

Step 3. Love Yourself

Being unhappy with life generally means you are unhappy with yourself and therefore struggle to love yourself. This normally stems from the necessity to put others before yourself or because a lack of self-confidence encourages us to focus on our faults and the things we dislike about ourselves.

If you can add a few of the healthy habits to love yourself into your life, you will start to notice that by taking care of yourself, everyday life becomes more positive. When you are able to love yourself, you might even start to see improvements in your relationship as your self-worth begins to increase. We will start off by looking at some of the easier ways to love yourself.

1. Keep a journal

Writing in a journal is an excellent outlet for your emotions and to let go of negative situations. It also helps you to process them and, afterward, concentrate your attention on the good parts and what you have learned from the experience. When you look back through your journal, you can be proud of how far you've come. I can't recommend keeping a journal enough because it gives you the chance to be completely honest about your feelings and not fear what other people think of you. A journal is a very significant tool to help you continue along the journey of self-discovery.

2. *Write down all of your achievements*

This is another tool that helps you focus only on the positive. A list of your accomplishments is a form of reminding yourself just how capable you are. Your completed list should then be celebrated, whether that's with others or by yourself. Be genuinely honest here, and don't be tempted to not add something to the list because it was someone else's idea or because you were helped by someone else.

Your achievements can include:

- Completing a project at work
- Starting/completing a new course
- Finishing a book
- Achieving a personal best in a sport
- Losing the weight you had hoped to

They will be different for everyone, but no achievement is too small for your list.

3. *Give yourself a physical and emotional break*

As a people pleaser, we often hold ourselves up to the assumed opinions and standards of others. When we don't meet this idea of perfection, we are just too hard on ourselves. Accept that certain things will happen, and that you can't be too hard on yourself.

On a similar note, it's important to give yourself physical breaks from the stress and strain of life. This is also quite a challenge for us because our time is often dedicated to others. This is why I recommend starting out with just five minutes a day and increasing it up to thirty minutes when you feel more comfortable. This time is solely for you. You might want to meditate, walk, read, or listen to music—as long as it's for you.

4. Enjoy time alone

I used to fear being alone; it was just empty time when I would dwell on the things I could have done differently or better. Now, I need it. It is important that you learn to like your own company in order to be able to love yourself. Being alone doesn't mean you are lonely. It gives you a chance to keep discovering new things that you like or dislike, experiences that you probably wouldn't do in the company of others.

5. Free yourself from your past mistakes

Everyone takes a walk down memory lane and ponders on the mistakes they have made, simply because there isn't a single human being that hasn't made some kind of mistake in their life. Looking at these mistakes can be a great opportunity to learn more about yourself. Nevertheless, in order to love yourself, you have to forgive yourself for the past and move on.

6. Travel

This might be the most difficult, but it is the most amazing experience, and once you travel for the first time, you will definitely want to repeat. Traveling alone allows you learn about yourself on a different scale because you are in various locations and, hopefully, diverse cultures. Being by yourself allows you to be true to yourself without having to be concerned about the feelings and thoughts of others.

Learning to love yourself is so crucial, and a step that you should and can start right now. All you need is your own mind and will. You don't need to fear the opinions of anybody else, and there is no need to worry about upsetting people. In fact, nobody will even see you taking these steps.

This was an amazing sensation for me, knowing that I was making tiny changes straight away. Knowing that none of my friends or family had to know about it meant I didn't have to fear the repercussions, and this let me explore more about myself. Most of the tips to love yourself will become a part of who you are, blended into your daily routine. Others may not occur as often, but even fifteen years later, I keep a journal, and a list of my achievements are written on the back. I also travel once a year, whether it's a weekend trip locally or a week somewhere overseas. When people ask if they can come with me, I smile and politely say, "No, not this time."

Step 4. Make Your Needs a Priority

We live in a world where it seems uncharitable or selfish to put your own needs ahead of others. Some people seem to do this with great ease, while the majority have to learn. People pleasing makes it damn near impossible, and although the theory is easy to grasp, putting it into practice is more of a challenge. First, let's appreciate why you have to learn how to prioritize your needs.

If you can't put your needs ahead of others, you run the risk of burning out and having nothing left to give. If everybody wants you to help them, you will spread yourself so thin that you will be so exhausted that you can't help anyone. It reminds me of how on an airplane, you should always put your oxygen mask on first before trying to help others. Equally as important, but a people pleaser might brush this one under the rug, you deserve to look after your own needs and to be happy.

When I began researching solutions for this habit, I was amazed at how many people said, "Learn to say no," and while this is something we will be able to do, I wanted something I could practice now. This is my advice on how to start making your needs a priority without jumping straight into using the no word.

Say yes to yourself: A little favorite of mine. After so long saying yes to others and no to myself, I turned the tables. We always have the ability to say no to ourselves in order to say yes to others. Now, even if it's just once in a while, say yes to yourself.

Find ways to save time: We all have little habits in the day that waste time, maybe a game on your phone or social media. If you can eliminate those things, then you will free up some time that you can devote to yourself.

Create a to-do list: Be careful not to fill your list with things that other people need you to do. Make sure you include one thing that you want to do (not *have* to do).

Use the time you have saved to do your task: You might be tempted to make a quick phone call to make sure your friend is okay, or run an errand for a colleague, but don't. You have freed up some of your time, and it should be just for you.

Create a daily routine: On some occasions, we will want to break out of the routine, but in the early stages, creating a routine will give you a better chance of getting to your needs because, from the very beginning, they are part of your routine.

Adjust your mindset: Again, this one might be more difficult, but it still doesn't require you to say no to anyone. When feelings of guilt arise, take a few slow deep breaths and replace the guilt with reminding yourself that you deserve to put your needs first.

Dedicate one day a month to you: Once you begin to allow time for yourself each day, it becomes easier to imagine having a whole day to yourself. This day (or start off with half a day) should be a combination of things that you need to do and want to do for yourself.

Step 5. Create a Personal Mantra

A mantra is a few words or a short sentence that you repeat in order to encourage a different behavior. They can be designed both for emotional and physical use, but our intention is to use them to adjust some of our habits.

A mantra or affirmation is a powerful way to start changing your mentality, and the results are visible within a very short time. By repeating your mantra, you send positive thoughts and energy to your mind that will lead to the mental changes you require and desire. You can find plenty of inspiration online or you can create your own mantra.

People pleasing is caused by a mental and emotional need to please others to whatever extent. We push our own needs and feelings to the back of our minds. The idea of a mantra is to free yourself from guilt, and the idea that you are not as worthy as those around you.

Here are some examples of mantras that can hack the mindset of a people pleaser:

- You have a lot of worth
- My needs matter
- I deserve happiness
- I am strong
- I am happy
- My dreams are important
- I am still a good person
- I respect myself

Notice that these short sentences don't contain any negative words, and they are not talking about the future. They are designed to remind both your conscious and subconscious of the changes you want now.

Mantras and affirmations can be used to start your day with a positive, firm mentality, or before going to bed to help calm your mind and help with a good night's sleep, or both. I found my mantra advantageous when people pleasing feelings began, for example, in situations where I wanted to say no but still brought myself to say it.

These five small habits have proven to be real game changers for myself and clients. They don't require tremendous effort, but they do produce almost instant results. You will find some of them harder than others, but I have purposely listed them in an order which I found easier to the more challenging.

Right now, you will probably find that going on vacation by yourself will be too much, too soon. You might feel obliged to tell others and to explain your reasons. At this point, you may not want to discuss overcoming your people pleasing with others, trying to explain why you are going away if it will make you uncomfortable, especially if your loved ones are concerned and try to talk you out of it. This is why we start off small in creating changes that will impact our lives and allow us to move on to the next stage.

The tips we have discussed are all excellent methods to help you continue your progress and build your way up to saying no. Once you start to feel the benefits of these hacks, you will find that you are better prepared for creating boundaries within your relationships and other areas of your life. Our next step is to understand the purpose of boundaries and how to create them. We are also about to learn how to control our fear of rejection, which is one of the major concerns we have at just the thought of saying no.

4

How to Set Healthy Boundaries without Fear

Boundaries are crucial for everybody, but more so for people pleasers. Without boundaries, our lives are a sea of gray. It is important for us to be able to please others, and we will continue to do so as the gray never ends. A boundary is the line between black and white, the line that reminds us of limits in terms of mental and emotional strain. For a people pleaser, a boundary is a way of caring for ourselves and showing us what we can and can't do, and what we should and shouldn't do for others.

Without having boundaries, a people pleaser will continue to make up excuses in order to be liked, feel accepted, and ensure others are happy. Not having a boundary in place makes it easier to forget or ignore our own needs in favor of others. As we sacrifice our own personalities in order to receive the affection we seek, we slowly remove any boundaries we ever had, if we had them to begin with.

What Is a Boundary?

A boundary is a divider of spaces. It can separate physical spaces or it can separate your emotions and values from those of others. It is about what you feel is acceptable in a certain situation. A boundary can also let others know how you expect to be treated.

Physical boundaries are often related to contact. You may have noticed that, in the world, there are huggers and non-huggers. When the two meet, the hugger will overstep the non-hugger's boundary and give them a warm embrace. The hugger sees no wrong in this whereas the non-hugger is beyond uncomfortable.

Emotional boundaries are those limits we set regarding our feelings. An example would be a friendly joke or mick-take. The person making the joke sees it as harmless fun, and it may well start out this way, but as soon as the joke steps over the boundary, the victim is hurt.

If the hugger and the joker were aware of other people's personal boundaries, the other parties wouldn't have felt that the imaginary line had been crossed. Just like when we looked at the roots of people pleasing, we aren't looking to place blame. Each individual is responsible for their own actions (i.e., the hug or the joke), but it is also important that we are cognizant of our boundaries and not scared to tell others about them.

Examples of Healthy and Unhealthy Boundaries

I am purposely leaving off the ability to say no as a healthy habit because there is no need to state the obvious. We are aware of our unhealthy boundary and are making excellent progress to overcome this. Instead, let's look at some other examples of healthy and unhealthy boundaries.

Healthy Boundaries

- Not compromising your personal values and/or beliefs
- Being able to express your emotions without fear
- Appreciating your own self-worth
- Respecting other people's feelings, beliefs, and perspectives
- Reading a social setting before potentially overstepping a line

Unhealthy Boundaries

- Sacrificing what you believe in so that you feel part of the group
- Hiding your emotions or feeling responsible for the way others feel
- Putting the self-worth of others above yours
- Showing disrespect or insulting opinions you don't agree with
- Inappropriate touching, whether of a sexual nature or not

Imagine each of your relationships as a set of scales with your values and opinions on one side, and the values and opinions of another person on the other side. In order for the relationship to be balanced, there needs to be a set of boundaries that each person is aware of and respects.

Unfortunately, people pleasers struggle to set boundaries because they don't place enough importance on their own feelings and what they want from life. Narcissists are known for overstepping boundaries, and people pleasers are often surrounded by such people, not necessarily because they intend to abuse the relationship, but because they are unaware of our boundaries. And this makes sense as we can't expect others to be aware of our boundaries when we haven't clearly defined them.

If you want others to respect your boundaries, then the first step is to understand what you consider to be acceptable behavior within a relationship that will allow you to feel safe. These boundaries should reduce the circumstances in which you need to say no because those who care about you will be more conscious of your needs and what you can and want to do. The result will be a blissful sensation of not having a million things to do for others and not having to worry about upsetting the dynamics of a relationship.

Each type of relationship will require a different set of boundaries, so let's take a look at some steps to follow so that we can work on creating various healthy boundaries within our relationships.

How to Set Healthy Boundaries for Your Friendships

Friendships rely heavily on unconditional love and communication. We choose our friends, sometimes at a young age and we grow up together, while other friends we meet along the way. Anyone who truly loves you for who you are will understand why you are choosing to set boundaries in your friendship, and they will respect your decision and even encourage you. This is because they sincerely value your happiness.

At the same time, setting boundaries in a friendship may lead you to discover who your real friends actually are. Those who disrespect your choice to have boundaries are already effectively breaking a boundary. Only you can decide who you should surround yourself with. But my advice is to use these exercises to strongly consider the honest foundations of your friendships and start breaking ties with people who aren't willing to appreciate your new, healthy boundaries.

Go back in time and look at the history of your friendship. Do you notice any recurring pattern where your friend has upset you or made you uncomfortable throughout your relationship? If so, setting boundaries based on these past situations will strengthen your relationship.

Understand what your body is telling you. Sometimes our stomach gets in a knot when a stressful situation comes up between you and your friend. When specific symptoms appear at just the thought of doing something with this friend, it is time to take a step back and identify what needs to change.

Mentally prepare yourself to talk to your friend. It's natural for us to shy away from this conversation because we will be nervous about the consequences. Keep telling yourself that you aren't doing anything wrong. You aren't about to tell them that you don't care about them, but just that you need to focus more on yourself. Remind yourself that this isn't selfish and that you want to improve the relationship you have.

- Choose the right time to talk to your friend about your new boundaries. The most suitable time is when they have crossed the line, perhaps turned up at your house too late or continued to talk about their own problems for too long. It will be easier for your friend to see your point of view and respect the new boundaries.

- Choose your vocabulary wisely. Try to avoid harsh words like, "I hate it when…," as this can lead to conflict and negative emotions to evolve into anger. Instead, start your conversation with words like, "I would feel more comfortable if we…".
- Discuss with your friend the fears you have when talking about your emotions. As a people pleaser, you will probably spend the majority of the time listening to their problems. This could be because they aren't used to you wanting to talk about how you feel rather than realizing that you fear their reaction. A simple conversation with a true friend about your fears will balance out the "therapy sessions" so that you have a chance to talk about your emotions too.
- Gently let your friends know if they do something that upsets you. People showing up late has always frustrated me, since it makes me feel as though they don't value my time. But I never had the confidence to tell anyone. I found it helped to first tell a friend in a kind of relaxed way with a smile. For example, "You know it drives me crazy when you are late." There was no need for me to get angry. The next time we made a plan, I followed up with, "You're not going to be late, are you?" The problem was solved, and I learned that sometimes we fear the worst with our friends, but those who love us don't want to do things that hurt us.

Finally, start with a friend who you have more faith in, someone who will be more understanding and respectful of the boundaries you wish to create. This will build up your confidence for friends who may need a firmer hand when it comes to respecting your boundaries.

How to Set Healthy Boundaries for Family Relationships

In many ways, the relationships with our family can be more complex than with our friends. There may have been times of stress, broken families, deaths, issues with money, or simply clashes of personalities that have gone unresolved in the past. It is harder to break free from the family relationships that don't function. For a people pleaser, we become more submissive and let others act and speak how they want so as not to rock the boat further.

We can apply some of the methods in order to create healthy family relationships. You will know what triggers your negative emotions in family situations, so you need to be aware of the anxiousness or even the sickness feeling that starts in the pit of your stomach. Perhaps it's the obnoxious aunt who compares you to your cousins, or the sibling who sees everything as a competition. Regardless of what your triggers are, make a mental note of them so that you know what boundaries need to be set.

Similarly, you need to remember that it is okay for you to put your needs ahead of your family's needs. And continue to remind yourself of this as you prepare for the conversation you will inevitably have to have.

Something else, which I did before talking to my family, was finding a way to cope with the feelings that arose when they overstepped the boundaries I wanted to create. I did this because I was more anxious about my family's reactions than those of my friends. I felt more worried about how my family would feel and how they would look at me. I also knew that any negative comeback from my family would lead to more anger and frustration, even if I wasn't able to show it.

For this reason, I started to practice some coping mechanisms a few weeks prior talking to my family. Each time I felt one of my boundaries was being overstepped, I would turn to my coping mechanism to relieve my pent-up anger. For me, this was doodling on a piece of paper on my balcony, preferably as the fresh, night-time air cooled me down.

You may want to consider some of these coping mechanisms as preparation for your conversations with your family about boundaries:

- Shouting/screaming into a pillow
- Listening to your favorite music and dancing
- Taking a hot bath or shower
- Exercising
- Meditation, mindfulness, yoga
- Getting a massage or spoiling yourself

Again, I started to introduce my new boundaries with an "easier" family member. I was never going to call a family meeting for fear of them all ganging up on me. I also made sure that the time was right, so I didn't call her and tell her that we needed to talk because I didn't want her getting worked up. I ended up talking to her as we were loading the dishwasher together one night.

I chose my mom because she was the easiest to talk to and because when I allowed her, she was a wonderful listener. Just remember that with some family members, they may be so concerned about you that the idea of you needing boundaries can upset them and almost make them feel guilty for what they have put you through.

I only want to highlight this so you are aware of what may happen when setting boundaries with your family members. This is certainly not a reason for you not to do it. It was just one of the situations where I needed to use a coping mechanism while I allowed my mom to process the fact that I wasn't happy with my life. From then on, I only had to smile and say, "Mom, remember our little conversation," any time our new imaginary line looked as if it was about to be crossed, and bless her, every time she would respond with a, "Yes, yes, you are right, dear."

It is unlikely you will be able to free yourself from family members who don't respect your boundaries. Nevertheless, with time and by practicing the steps in this book, you will be able to say no to the situations that lead to family members overstepping your boundaries.

How to Set Healthy Boundaries in the Workplace

Work relationships can be even more complex than friendships and our family bonds. When it comes to our jobs, we have no choice but to spend an average of eight hours a day with our colleagues. Even if you work from home, you still need to work closely with those in the office. In this case, while physical boundaries are easier to cope with, there are still plenty of other lines that can be crossed.

On top of this, due to employment retention, it is common for people to come and go and, quite often, and there may not be enough time to develop strong relationships with colleagues so that you feel comfortable expressing your boundaries.

For those without people pleasing personalities, it is easier for them to bring up violations of boundaries as soon as they occur. For a people pleaser, the fluctuations with staff coming and going can make defining boundaries even harder.

For this reason, I like to carry out an initial assessment of the people I (or my clients) are working with, and we separate them into two groups: those we have been working with for a while and feel that we could discuss boundaries with, and those with whom we are still developing a working relationship.

If you have had the time to work with someone for months or even years, you will probably have established the foundations of your working relationship and may have even developed a friendship. So, I would advise you to follow the steps in creating boundaries with your friends but combine this with some coping strategies that we used with our families, though you may have to adjust some for the working environment.

The reason this combination works well is because we have to learn to cope with these emotions as soon as we begin to feel them so that they do not escalate. You can walk away from someone in your family or a friend and take time to cool down. However, you will likely suffer the consequences of walking away from work.

For the new colleagues, one would initially fear this the most. But I see this as the perfect opportunity to put what you have learned into practice straight away without the fear of hurting those you love:

- Let people know your values as soon as they come up in conversation. Your values are what you should never sacrifice, more so now because it can speak to your work ethic.
- If you feel confident, you can share your opinions from the very beginning. Alternatively, introduce your opinions with the right vocabulary, emphasizing the team environment, for example, "Perhaps it would be better if we considered…"
- Ensure that others know your schedule from day one. Knowing your boundaries, for example that they can't reach you between certain hours, means they will be less likely to cross those lines.
- Justify your explanations without "fluff." A positive for the people pleasers is that emotional justifications are often useless in the workplace. Telling someone you can't do something only makes it about you. When the attention is turned back to the project, your boundary is well-defined but with a logical reason, for example, "If I do 'X,' I won't be able to do 'Y' and the client is relying on this."

How to Set Healthy Boundaries in Your Romantic Relationships

It's like a trifecta. The person you are probably closest too, your best friend, and the person you spend the most time with. Unhealthy boundaries in a relationship will mean that you don't feel complete without them, or you depend on them to do things. You may even feel like your life wouldn't be happy without them.

You might let your partner get away with things you don't like, such as messing up your recently cleaned kitchen or borrowing your car without asking. You may even change your plans, so you don't disturb their plans. I had a client that stopped watching her favorite TV program because her boyfriend needed his afternoon nap.

None of the above may be enough for the relationship to end, but if you look closely, is it a balanced relationship? Boundaries in a partnership or marriage are essential for a balance between your priorities, and they empower you to make the changes you need, preventing further conflict so that neither you nor your partner get hurt.

Here are six things you should consider when planning the boundaries you want to see in a partnership.

1. Allow space and freedom for you both to do what you want to do.
2. Take responsibility for the tasks that need to be carried out at home.

3. Love your partner through the good times and the bad but know when to admit enough is enough if their behavior crosses a line you cannot tolerate.
4. Learn to forgive if boundaries are overstepped, but again, only those words or actions that don't go against your emotions or beliefs.
5. Be honest and give your partner a chance to be truthful.
6. Once you are clear on your boundaries, make sure your partner is fully aware of them and then confidently stick to them. I know this is hard, but it is essential for your relationship and your happiness.

Relationships can fall under so many categories when combined with an almost infinite number of personality combinations. Some people decide drug abuse is an absolute boundary that should never be crossed, while others will never recover from infidelity.

Creating your boundaries is an individual task. The steps above are guidelines that will work for a wide range of relationship boundaries, but the intricate details are for you to determine based on what matters most to you. Remember that if you have been in a relationship for a long time, it is hard to make any form of change. We become comfortable in the rules we have set, even if the rules are unfair. It's okay to seek help and use the tips in this book.

For long-term relationships, you may face a different set of challenges. Your partner might not understand why the sudden need for change. In these cases, try the following tips:

How to Set Healthy Boundaries without Fear

1. Choose a time when you are both in a happy place, not after a different, difficult discussion or after a long hard day.
2. Make sure the moment is right and that there are no interruptions.
3. Explain the changes you require. It isn't because they have done something wrong; it's just that you need to be happier, and you want your relationship to have more meaning.
4. Be very honest about your emotions, but keep the vocabulary focused on your feelings and not about how your partner makes you feel.
5. Include suggestions for ways that you can continue to grow together, create new shared goals, or suggest new experiences for you to both learn from together.
6. Remind them that your feelings toward them haven't changed, and that you still love them.

While it might be challenging to make the changes after being together for so long, the conversation will hopefully be easier because you should be able to express yourself better now.

Overcoming Your Fear of Rejection

Half of what stops us from setting boundaries is that we don't want to let others down, and the other half is because we fear what may happen when someone doesn't accept our boundaries and may reject us because of this.

We are social beings. We need to feel closeness and connection by being in contact with others. The fear of rejection stems from early mankind when being rejected from a tribe would impact our chance of survival. Fear of rejection is another emotion that is natural for everyone but affects people pleasers more profoundly.

Modern technology has made the fear of rejection so much worse. We send a text message, and we see the tick showing that it has been received and read, but then there is no reply. Our minds aren't capable of going to the logical explanation, like the other person is just busy. Rather, we assume it must be a sign of rejection.

One of the things I discovered is how our fear of rejection and the fear of the word no is so closely related, and yet so distinct. When a sales representative pitches a new product and the client says no, they feel rejected. We have taken the word no as a personal attack, but in reality, the client only said no to the product.

When our friend or partner says no to a night out, we begin to think they don't want to spend time with us, and we feel rejected. Really, it is more likely that they are tired or would just prefer a nice meal on the sofa together.

Before we go over exercises to overcome the fear of rejection, it is essential to understand that at some point in our lives, we will feel rejected. It could be the end of a job or relationship, a short-term period like when someone doesn't reply to a message, or not even a personal rejection, but a no to an idea or object. It is perfectly normal and should in no way be taken personally. Instead, take advantage of the following exercises:

How to Set Healthy Boundaries without Fear

1. Learn from your experience. If you have applied for a job and you didn't get it, the first thing that hits you is the wave of rejection. Allow yourself to process this, but for no more than a minute, then decide what you did right and what you could have done better. Ask for feedback.

2. Though you can mentally prepare for rejection, you shouldn't allow yourself to expect it. If you do, you start to see rejection in places where it doesn't exist.

3. If someone has said no to you, don't dwell on it. You might be tempted to start with the, "If only I had...," but it really isn't worth it as you are turning the blame back onto yourself.

4. Go back to your journal. Flip through your entries and remind yourself of your worth. Look over your achievements, your goals and the progress you have made.

5. Talk to those you love. Now that your new boundaries are in place, it is time to start taking the opportunity to talk to them about how you feel after what appears to be a personal rejection.

6. Remember that at some point, everyone gets rejected. It's important not to take it personally. In most cases, people are rejecting an idea or a suggestion, and they are not rejecting you as a person.

7. Find the positive in the rejection. Imagine you are in sales, and you have to pitch a new idea to one of your clients that absolutely loves to talk through every detail

endlessly. If this client says no, there is a positive here. You won't have to waste numerous hours dealing with a difficult client. Quite often, when we start to look for the positives, rejection may even seem like the better outcome.

8. Create more self-confidence. Sometimes in friendships and relationships, people just don't gel. This doesn't mean that the relationship has failed because of something you have done or that you have been rejected. Write a list of the best attributes about yourself, and what you can contribute to a friendship or relationship.

9. Put things in perspective. If you suggest a family day out, but others would rather have a BBQ at home, isn't the most important thing that you are spending time together?

10. Understand where your fear is coming from. If you fear rejection from a loved one, it might be because you can't stand the idea of being lonely, so you can work on strengthening the other relationships in your life. This might not always be sufficient to overcome your fear, but it might be enough for you to take baby steps, or at least make yourself more aware.

11. Face your fears. It is scary, but just because you fear something might happen, it doesn't guarantee it will. If you ask someone on a date, they may say no, but there is also a chance they say yes. Think what you could miss out on because of fear that something that may not happen. When facing your fears, you should

also consider taking small steps. Break the fear down so that it becomes easier to manage. Separate it into who, what, when, where, and why, then tackle each one individually.

12. Focus on other things you will gain. Let's say you hoped to qualify for a course or degree. Although you didn't get into the course you wanted to, the administration pointed out several other courses you weren't aware of, some actually more suitable. Every situation where you face rejection will offer you something, even if it's just more courage.

13. Every no brings you closer to a yes. It's not just the law of averages, but every time you learn something from being rejected, you can apply this to become better, taking you a little closer to a yes.

14. Never hesitate. If you start to tell yourself that there will be a better moment, you are allowing the fear to take control of you. This fuels the situation, breathing more fear into the rejection that might not even be there.

15. Concentrate on how you want to feel. We quickly jump to how we don't want to feel, though it is more productive if we concentrate on how we want to feel. If you are faced with rejection, determine how you want to handle the situation. Tell yourself you want to be positive, and that you want to learn from the experience.

16. Visualize yourself handling rejection in a confident way, without it upsetting you and causing you to doubt yourself.

17. Look to your idols for inspiration. Most people have an actor who they like and/or admire. It is highly likely that at some point they have been rejected and have not only survived, but have gone on to accomplish amazing things, just like you can. Harrison Ford, Steven Spielberg and Hugh Jackman are just some examples.
18. Have faith in your ability to get back up again. If someone says no, you may feel horrible for a few minutes, or hours, maybe a day. But in one week from now, will the no still have the same significance? Or will you have gained something better? Either way, you are strong enough to survive.

This chapter has been quite full of ideas to take you one step further out of your comfort zone. The previous chapter looked at mental hacks that didn't require others to be a part of your progress. At this point, you have created a clear idea of your boundaries, and how you are going to introduce them into your daily life. You also now have the tools behind you to overcome the fear of rejection. Along the way, you will discover more about your relationships, and some of this will be a great relief and encourage you to continue. Other discoveries might make you appreciate who should be in your life and who it is time to say goodbye to.

Process all that you have learned so far. Remember not to rush it and to move at the pace you feel comfortable with. Feel positive that you are gaining momentum, and you are well on your way to learning how to say no.

5

Start Saying No in Seconds without Feeling Guilty

The time has come for you to finally overcome what you once thought would be impossible. This chapter will not only teach you how to say no, but also when to use this mighty word. We will also look at the beauty of saying yes, not because you have to, but because you want to.

The stages that we have been working on up to now have been preparing us for this moment, and by now you will probably have a clearer understanding of when you want to say no. The journey to self-discovery highlighted our goals and what we want and need from life to be happy. We learned a few tips to begin the progress and to start seeing positive changes. And now that we have clearly defined our boundaries and made those we love aware of them, it's time to take action when people overstep the mark.

And people will overstep the mark. Normally, this is no fault of their own. A sudden rush of emotions encourages them to call on you when it's not the right time, or they are too insistent because they are convinced you will enjoy the experience. Let's reinforce our understanding of when to say no.

- Think about how you feel in this situation: are you angry, nervous, or perhaps you feel calm? Are your feelings about the proposal positive?
- Consider your priorities and whether you realistically have the time to say yes. If you already have too much on your plate, you will need to say no.
- Check that none of your boundaries are being pushed to the limit.
- If you aren't ready to make a decision, request more time.

The last point is vital for us, but only when used in the right way and when we are honest about our feelings. For example, if your feelings are mixed, and you like the idea and could change a few plans to fit in the activity, then you genuinely can tell the person that you will get back to them with an answer. This provides you with further time to make sure you can look at all of the options and make the right decision. However, if you don't want to do something, if the word no is on the tip of your tongue, but you can't find the courage to say it, don't ask for more time. You are only delaying the inevitable.

Another solution is to ask for advice when you're unsure of whether to say yes or no. This is particularly useful in the workplace. This is perfect if you aren't certain of what someone is asking you to do is realistic or could potentially jeopardize other areas of your job. Again, a simple sentence like, "Let me get back to you on that," will give you the time you need to not feel rushed into a response. Once the pressure is relieved, you won't feel forced into saying yes on the spot.

Start Saying No in Seconds without Feeling Guilty

How to Say No

There are three key rules when you feel the need to say no. They are short, sharp, and simple, and I find that repeating these rules before I say no, or even throughout the day, keeps my mentality stronger.

1. Saying no isn't easy.
2. I am in control of my time.
3. One no is a yes for me.

It's not just that this word is difficult for us, it can be absolutely terrifying. I was also worried that the other person would see my fear and laugh at me. Though this isn't easy, the first no is always the hardest. You are going to have to step out of your comfort zone. But when you say it for the first time, you will feel a mad sensation of pride, satisfaction, and a sense of achievement.

Reminding yourself that you are in control of your own time and happiness is a great way to feel like you have more control over the conversation, and then the thought of you doing something you actually want to do should be enough to motivate you to say no.

Once you have assessed the situation, and you are ready to say no, you should:

- Say no politely, and with a smile on your face; offer an apology along with your no.
- Be assertive without being aggressive.
- Don't become the victim of peer pressure and ignore sentences like, "But everyone else is."

- Stand your ground and remember your boundaries.
- If the person is persistent, stay strong, allow yourself to be selfish with your time, and repeat the no.

Learning how to be assertive without being aggressive requires improving your verbal and non-verbal communication skills. It is about choosing the right words, for example, instead of saying, "Do this," which is aggressive, you can say, "Start." Phrases like, "That's a stupid idea," are just aggressive and will only cause negative feelings. Assertive behavior would encourage further ideas without insulting those who have made suggestions. Shouting and interrupting will not achieve anything except fear, so it is important to make sure you are loud enough to be heard, without needing to shout. Also, too much eye contact makes you feel like the person is trying to stare you down rather than assert themselves.

It is quite an extensive topic, so we have dedicated a chapter to this a little further on.

Powerful No Sentences That Are Polite Yet Firm:

- "No, I'm sorry, today is absolutely impossible."
- "I would love to, but I am already stretched too thin."
- "No, I'm sorry, I already have other commitments."
- "Thank you, I appreciate the offer, but I have plans."
- "No, but I wish I could. It sounds amazing, so hopefully next time."

Notice how none of these responses give any explanation for your no. You don't need to justify your answer any more than they would have to if you were to ask a question.

In a wonderful world, the person will accept your no and move on. Having said that, they will probably be used to you saying yes to everything and, being taken aback, they will continue to try to change your mind.

In many ways, this is harder than the initial no. The confidence and control we had prepared ourselves with starts to be overpowered by the feeling of letting people down. In your mind, the quickest way to get out of this awful situation is just to say yes. However, it is absolutely crucial that you do not say yes.

Anyone who has ridden a horse knows that the moment you fall off, you jump straight back on again as if you were Billy the Kid. If you start to look at the horse, you become nervous and back away. If you tell yourself you will get back on tomorrow, it is possible that you will never ride again.

Our persistent person is the horse, and the minute you say yes, you run the risk of never being able to say no. On the other hand, if you stand your ground, this person will learn that you have boundaries which are not to be broken, and the next time you have to say no, they won't try to twist your arm.

They may ask you the reason behind your no, and again, this is a boundary that shouldn't be overstepped as everyone is entitled to some privacy. Look at the two different scenarios:

A: Can you work overtime tonight?
B: No, sorry, I can't.

A: Why?
B: 1) Because I have another engagement.
2) Because it's my grandmother's birthday, and I promised I would go and visit.

Option one leaves no 'wiggle room.' Option two could lead the person to delve further into your personal life, telling you that granny has had loads of birthdays, and she can wait a while and to visit her later, or worse, psychological mind games such as, "Granny will be happy knowing you are doing a great job at work." This type of sentence appeals to a people pleaser because it makes us feel appreciated and that we are needed. Nevertheless, it's not a genuine compliment. It is always best avoid giving reasons or personal bits of information.

The best way to handle those who don't take no for an answer is to offer them an alternative. When a friend wants you to go to the cinema, and they keep being persistent, remain firm but suggest a different activity. It is possible they will say no to your idea, but it will start a little brainstorming session on the best option for both of you.

For a work-related alternative, suggest a time you would be able to fulfill the other person's needs. If you can't work overtime that night, you could suggest the following day.

Alternatives are not a sign of you backing down because you have stuck to your original no. They can be used as a method of compromise so that the other person is still happy, and you aren't forced into doing something you don't want to, or you just don't have time for.

When to Say Yes

Learning to say no doesn't mean that you won't be able to say yes. What it does mean is that when you say yes, you will know in your heart that you mean it and that you honestly want to spend time or help the person who is asking you. Saying yes once you have learned to say no is like that moment when you breathe the fresh, crisp air after a storm. It's peaceful and at the same time, energizing.

Choosing when to say yes is down to your personal circumstances. You will need to take a deep look at your feelings about the question, analyze your available time, and ultimately decide if saying yes is going to make you happy.

If these three things aren't ticked off, you need to go back to giving yourself some time to think about it further. Use sentences like, "I would love to, but I might have to rearrange a few things," and, "Can I get back to you?" Let's look at an example.

Say you have promised your mom that you will help her in the garden on Saturday, but your friends also want you to go on a day trip. Neither option fills you with dread and, in fact, they both sound quite fun. It's impossible to split yourself in two, and so you will have to say no to someone.

Spending some time with your mom will make you happy. You know she will cook your favorite lunch and tackling the garden will be rewarding. Spending time with your friends and going somewhere new will be a break from the routine. If you want to do both, you could try offering both parties an alternative. Could Mom do the gardening on Sunday or could the friends make it the weekend after?

Or what if your boss wants you to attend a course and saying yes will provide you with amazing opportunities to grow? You should say yes, providing it doesn't require you to miss out on other activities that will make you happy, or overwhelm you with too much to do already.

Your yes answer should never come from a fear of rejection or guilt. Take the time to decide if the option is good for you. Understand where your fear is coming from. If it is a fear of trying something new or learning more about yourself, you should probably say yes as the rewards will be worth it.

How to Stop Feeling Guilty

Guilt is the emotion that rises up when we feel like we have done something wrong. Emphasis on the "feel like" since it doesn't imply that we have done something wrong. People pleasing and saying no makes us feel guilty, even though the only thing we have done wrong is prioritize our needs.

According to the American Psychiatric Association, excessive or inappropriate guilt is a symptom of clinical depression. It may stem from a number of causes including post-traumatic stress disorder, childhood trauma, or even survivor's guilt.

Guilt can also be considered healthy if we are able to use it in order to find motivation, or to fix a wrong that we may have committed.

We are going to concentrate on the unhealthy, unjustified guilt that eats away at people pleasers. The guilt that takes over us appears for a number of reasons. Saying no means hurting someone's feelings. We say no to our children in the hope of bringing them up with stronger morals, but they are too young to see this. We feel guilty because we could be doing more for our friends and family, even though you sacrifice the majority of time for them, but you still feel that you should do more. Or we feel guilty because we chose to do an activity with someone, and it meant we had to say no to someone else.

If you look at it from a non-people pleaser perspective, how do you think they feel? Some years ago, we had a party and my niece was away with her dad. I felt terrible that she was going to miss out. Her mom said, "Yes, it's a shame, but she will get over it and there will be more parties." I learned a valuable lesson on the difference between appreciating the pity or shame of a situation and letting it continue to attack mentally.

Self-care guilt is a serious problem for those who feel the need to make others happy. Self-care is about looking after ourselves physically and emotionally, and it is a necessity for our well-being. It isn't anything selfish, but we think that dedicating time to look after ourselves is time we could have spent doing things for others, and this leads to even more guilt.

This is why we have talked about the importance of creating a routine that allows for 'me-time.' If you can take thirty minutes a day, and one day a month reserved only for looking after yourself, the time has already been allocated and therefore you won't feel guilty about not doing something for someone else.

Making it part of your routine makes it natural. So, if you want to start removing feelings of guilt, you have to know how much you can handle and the boundaries you have in place.

Here are five more exercises that will stop you from feeling guilty:

1. *Find the evidence that your guilt is justified.*

If your friend tells you that you never do anything together, look back and see if this is true. If it has been a while since you spent some time together, then you can fix it. If they are exaggerating the situation, it means that there is no real evidence for your guilt.

2. *Use your journal for self-gratification.*

Since we have a tendency to forget our accomplishments, a lot of guilt is brought on because of the things that we can't do. Write a list of everything you have managed to do for others as well as yourself. This will remind you that you are actually a very generous and loving person and it will prevent you from feeling guilty about the small acts you do for yourself.

3. *Stop being so hard on yourself.*

This is particularly true for women, who (as stated in the Spanish *Journal of Psychology*) are more prone to feelings of guilt. Take a look at what those around you accomplish in a day or a week. Have your kids or partner worked an eight-hour day, cleaned the house, and prepared dinner? Do they feel guilty for watching TV while you are still working?

4. Remind yourself that everyone makes mistakes.

I burned the dinner one night for six friends. It was a mistake, and I miscalculated the temperature, but I felt guilty that the whole night was ruined. There was no need for this guilt, and it was a genuine mistake. We ordered take out and the evening went on. Also, remind yourself that sometimes there is no right or wrong way to do something. If you choose to do something in a way you feel is right, it doesn't warrant you feeling guilty. It's your right to choose.

5. Think about what you will achieve from feeling guilty.

If it is something that you can put right, then the healthy guilt has served a valuable purpose. You can take responsibility for your mistake, you can learn from it, but it is in the past. Guilt is an emotion that is associated with our past actions, and once we have learned from the experience, there is little place for guilt in the future.

Saying no might be hard at first, but it is your right to do so, and it is essential that you don't feel selfish about putting your needs first for a change or for letting this make you feel guilty. There is a positive way you can say no to someone, and as seen in the examples, you can even turn down an idea without the word itself. Body language and offering alternatives are perfect ways to eliminate conflict and allow for a compromise so that both sides are happy and there is no need for you to feel guilty about letting anyone down.

I hope this chapter has stirred up some amazing emotions inside you. Learning when the right time is to say yes or no is an invaluable tool that leads to a much happier life. Now that you are aware of the feelings caused by situations, you will know in your heart and your gut what the right answer should be. Don't forget the importance of delaying an answer if you feel the need to take more time to reach the right decision.

If you haven't said your first no yet, that's okay. Remember, it is about the preparation and making sure it's the right moment so that you are more able to stand your ground. If you have, I hope you feel the same way I did, like the weight of the world had been lifted off your shoulders, and that you can start to see the light at the end of the tunnel.

There may be little bumps along your way, but this is normal, and there are still plenty of people pleasing tips and advice that will strengthen your abilities. While you continue to practice what you have learned so far, let's move on to the possible reactions from other people when you say no. It's these reactions that we may fear more than the actual declining, so it is necessary to prepare ourselves in order to stand tall, and be firm in saying no.

6

Dealing with People's Reactions

As mentioned at the end of the previous chapter, there will be a few bumps along the way, and this is absolutely fine. It is not a sign that you aren't overcoming your people pleasing problem, or that you will never have the ability to say no. This is a learning curve that will be full of experiences. Most will be amazingly positive, and a few will be negative, but every experience provides an opportunity to learn.

You might be surprised at the range of reactions you receive from people. You may see shock, surprise, or happiness that you are standing up for yourself. Other people may not like your newfound ability to put yourself first, which will lead them to feel angry or frustrated.

It is also very likely that you will spend a lot of time thinking about how someone is going to react before you even get to saying no. The thought will make you start to feel nervous and maybe even doubt your decision. The longer you spend going over the possible reactions of others, the more these nerves turn into anxiety. This anxiety becomes a part of a vicious circle that impacts our eating and sleeping habits, as well as other areas of our lives.

Anxiety is unhealthy and potentially dangerous. For this reason, we are going to take a little time to explore the anxiety we feel when we start to concern ourselves with other people's reactions.

How to Stay Calm and Stop the "What People Think" Anxiety

The first thing you should remember is that you will never be able to please everyone and that trying to will only set yourself up for failure. Imagine you have to give a presentation in front of twenty people. One person will be jealous because you were picked to do it over them. Another might snicker at what you are wearing, whereas the person next to them thinks your outfit is well chosen. Some smile at you encouragingly. In every situation you face, you will get mixed reactions. Even dealing with one person, you can get more than one.

Imagine the boss who says, "I'm disappointed but I understand." For a people pleaser, we won't take this as a win, rather we tend to focus on the fact that we have disappointed someone. However, other people's emotions and reactions are not our responsibilities, and we shouldn't feel guilty, just as our feelings are only our responsibility.

Steps to Facing "What People Think" Anxiety

1. Pay attention to the situation

We have established that the anxiety begins when we have to say no. The next is to ask which people trigger this feeling more than others. Your best friend might make you nervous whereas your colleague might take the feelings to a higher level of anxiety.

Then decide just how much power this person has over you. Your boss may have power because they have an impact on your career. Your colleague, on the other hand, doesn't have any real power over you. By answering these questions, you will be able to understand the best way to focus your mind.

2. Decide if your anxieties are warranted

Based on past experiences with people, you will have an expectation of how they may react. So many times, we build up an image in our head of how we think something is going to turn out, but it isn't warranted. We panic that mom is going to go crazy if we don't go to the family dinner, even though she never has in the past.

At times, we assume a situation is going to be far worse than it really is, which increases the anxiety. If you have never had any dealings with a person, and you aren't sure of their reactions, it's crucial not to assume their reaction will be a negative one.

3. Ask yourself why you care about the other person's reaction

You care because you want others to like you and think well of you. But what happens if saying yes doesn't cause this person to respect you, or even like you? The end result is that you have to do something you don't want to do, and the person thinks no better of you.

Even if this person holds you in high regard for agreeing with them, some will say this is a high price to pay, and there are better, more honest ways to gain respect.

4. Know where your anxiety comes from

Our feelings of worry and anxiety stem normally from feeling as if we are out of control, and more specifically, that you don't have the control over your decisions and how you live your life. Just like with emotions, you can't control how others view you.

If someone has made the decision not to like you, it is something out of your control, even with huge amounts of efforts to change that opinion.

Do you really need this person to like you? Are there not plenty of other people in the world who we can like and that can like us for who we really are?

If anxiety is coming from a lack of control, then you need to take control. In this situation, the best way to take control is to make the decision to walk away.

How to Stay Calm When You Feel Anxious

It is always best to handle your anxiety before approaching the subject of saying no because the worry and nervousness will only add to the stress of the situation. Here are five ways you can stay calm as soon as the panic makes a presence.

1. **Stand up:** The next time you get anxious, notice how the natural reaction is to become hunched. This is because we are protecting our heart and lungs. If you stand up, or at least sit upright, you will feel a better sense of self-control.

2. **Focus on your breathing:** Not just deep breathing but concentrate on inhaling and exhaling for the same amount of time. This will engage your mind and stop you from thinking about what has made you feel anxious.
3. **Change your activity:** If you are working and can't shake off the anxiety, walk away. Go to the photocopier, grab a piece of fruit, or do anything that takes you away from the place where you were having those thoughts.
4. **Don't reach for the sugar:** Chocolate might be your favorite comfort food, but the sugar rush can make the anxiety worse. Instead, go for something with more protein as this releases your energy slower.
5. **Play the 333 game:** This is a personal favorite for encouraging the brain to not think about your anxiety. Think of three things you can see, three things you can hear, and then three things you can smell. You can also choose anything to think of in threes that focuses the mind.

There are lots of other ways you can stay calm and prevent anxiety. You might find reading a book or watching funny videos good for taking your mind off of things, or you may prefer going for a walk. A quick phone call to a friend could also help calm you down. You can talk to them about how you feel and then turn the focus to something positive or make a plan for something to look forward to.

How to Deal with People When They Become Frustrated

It is upsetting when someone becomes frustrated when you say no to them. Both of you are hurting, but you are only responsible for how you feel, and you can only control your actions and opinions. Nevertheless, there are things that you can do to make the situation better.

An instant solution of stopping the other person from becoming frustrated is to say yes, but this is far from the ideal solution.

Our goal is to stand our ground, not back down on our values or allow our boundaries to be crossed, but to employ the following techniques so that the frustrated person doesn't get angry.

Build a rapport with the person

Avoid things like, "I know how you feel," since it opens the door to replies such as, "Well if you know how I feel, why don't you just do it." This is more about a rapport on a subconscious level. By mirroring the other person's actions (like standing up if they are), you enable them to make a connection with you.

Listen to what they are saying

Although you have said no to their suggestion, it doesn't mean that the conversation ends there. It is a good idea to see if there is some compromise to be had. Listen and even repeat the core parts of what they are saying. They will calm down knowing they have been heard.

Ask questions

Asking questions shows the other person that you are interested in finding a solution, and the chances are, they are frustrated because they can't think of an alternative. Asking questions is similar to brainstorming together, and it will take their mind off the fact that you have said no.

Suggest readdressing the issue at another time

When emotions start to get heated, it might be wiser for both parties to walk away but not to ignore the problem. Use phrases like, "How about we take an hour, and I will come back with some thoughts." The time apart will allow them to calm down while you can come up with some ideas that can solve the problem but not put you out of place.

People pleasers will rarely become frustrated or agitated because we are always looking for ways to keep the peace. That being said, if you start practicing your calming techniques while they are frustrated, you may cause the situation to become worse. Be calm and practical, but also be firm without being rude. Even though it might not seem so at the time, you will gain more respect in the long run.

Stop Manipulation Techniques

Manipulation is another trigger area for people pleasers. Part of healthy relationships is what is known as "social influence." This is when one person in a relationship influences another as part of the give-and-take. It could be anything from following a new trend or going to a party because everyone else is.

When it comes to manipulation, one person will have power over the other and they will use this to their benefit. The difficulty arises when we are unable to see the line between social influence and manipulation. As we feel the need to please others, we may not even see a line and just hope that we are able to make someone happy.

It is essential to learn how to identify when you are being manipulated before you can put a stop to this behavior. There are five key personality traits to a manipulator:

- Manipulators have a complex set of personal problems and history. This will cause them to run very hot and cold. They might be angelic one moment, then demonic the next.
- They are experts at discovering a person's weaknesses.
- They will use any weakness they find against you in order to benefit themselves.
- They have the skills to encourage you to give something up in order to improve their own situation.
- Once they have manipulated you for the first time, they won't stop until you force a change in the behavior.
- Manipulators are capable of using your feelings of guilt and the need to please against you.

Once you have identified a manipulator, and you can see that they are using you for their own gain, you have several options. The first is to keep your distance from them. You can't change

Dealing with People's Reactions

their behavior and their extreme emotions will not help your emotional health.

But if you have to deal with manipulators, try to make sure you are in an environment with others there. Manipulators are less likely to take advantage of you when there are witnesses. It also means that you are in a safe location in case they become angry or aggressive. In some situations, it would be wise to keep a record of any inappropriate behavior.

Normally, dealing with manipulation techniques is quite straightforward if you follow this guide:

- Remember your boundaries and that you have a right to your individual opinions and ideas, the right to prioritize your own needs, and the right to say no without feeling guilty.
- Manipulators have no respect for your boundaries, so you will have to be firmer with your no. Do not feel the need to apologize, but you should still be courteous. Stand tall and make eye contact.
- Reflect their request back on them. Ask them if they think their request sounds fair or reasonable. Ask what you gain from the situation, and whether or not you have a say in it. Although they are fully aware that they are manipulating you, if you put the focus back on them, they will probably notice you are aware of what they are doing.
- Steer clear of blame as you are not the cause of the situation. Instead, reaffirm your position by asking yourself if this person respects you, is there give-and-

take in your relationship, and whether their requests are appropriate.
- Take time to respond if you need it. Phrases like, "I'll get back to you," or, "I'll think about it," gives you a chance to step back from the situation and think about your feelings on how you are being treated.

Manipulators play on our need to make others happy. They know that we aren't happy, but that we will do it anyway. It's not the same as a true friend who might want to influence us to do something for our own benefit, such as trying a new restaurant. A manipulator will use techniques to pressure you into going to the restaurant knowing that the food is disgusting, but they are friends with the owner who needs the business.

We can try our hardest to keep manipulators out of our lives, but the sad fact is, they are everywhere, and we can't avoid them forever which is why we must learn how to spot and stop them.

Dealing with Intrusive People

When learning about intrusive people, I found it very interesting to go back to Byron Katie's work on the three businesses. It was used as a way to understand suffering in the world but is also frequently used to analyze how we tend to cross even more lines and get into other people's business.

The first business is the Business of God (if this sounds too religious for you, you can call it the Business of the Universe).

Dealing with People's Reactions

This refers to nature, the weather, the disasters that we have no control over, and the beauty in the world. Then there is your business, which is what you choose to do with your life, how you decide to act and behave. Finally, there is my business, the decisions and reasons why I choose to manage my life a certain way.

There are some people in the world who are unable to keep the boundaries between their business and the business of others. You can call them intrusive, nosy, even busy bodies, essentially, they are violating your boundaries by crossing into your business.

Intrusive people are rarely aggressive, and they don't want to manipulate you. On the other hand, when you say no, they will likely pry into the reasons for your answer. They may think that they know the best solution for you. Here are some examples of intrusive behavior:

- Your parents want you to go to your third cousin's wedding, but you haven't seen her for years, and you never really liked her. Instead of accepting no for an answer, your parents want to know what could possibly be more important.
- Your boss wants you to take on additional work, but you are already beyond overwhelmed with your work. You explain that it isn't possible, but they try to find ways to manage your time.
- Your friend wants to set you up with someone they adamantly know you will like.

In situations like the above, it is necessary that you don't feel obliged to give a reason to justify why you don't want to do something. A simple, "I have plans" or, "I am unavailable," will suffice. Offer alternatives if you prefer and then change the subject.

How to Handle Intrusive Strangers

When you don't know someone very well, some people find even basic questions intrusive, and this will depend on the boundaries you have set. When someone asks you a question you feel uncomfortable answering, avoid saying things like, "Mind your own business," as it comes off as aggressive. There are, however, ways to respond to questions you aren't inclined to answer.

- Make light of the question. If someone asks you how old you are, tell them you are young.
- Let people know you are uncomfortable with certain types of questions: "I'm not comfortable discussing politics."
- Turn the conversation back to them: "I would like to know more about you."
- Find out why they are asking such questions. If someone is asking you about your holiday to France, ask them where they heard about it. You might find you have a common friend and so you are more relaxed about discussing the topic.
- If people persist in their questions, don't hesitate in telling them how you feel. Let the person know that you feel uncomfortable or pressured.

Dealing with People's Reactions

Notice how all of the responses are in the first person, and we respond with "I." This is a good habit to get into for a few reasons. First of all, it lets others know more about the boundaries you have in place.

Also, it is a way of taking responsibility for your feelings toward such questions. When you answer with something like, "It's rude to ask someone their age," then it doesn't tell the other person clearly that you are uncomfortable. Instead, you are only stating what is socially correct or incorrect.

It might seem we are rehashing old dogs here, but when learning to deal with other people's reactions, it is crucial you always bear in mind that their feelings and reactions are nothing for you to feel guilty about, or to feel you have any control over. You know your boundaries, and a lot of dealing with other people's reactions is about letting them know where your limits are. It also helps if you can remain firm yet calm, and use the techniques provided to instill a sense of calm in the situation.

Now that we have covered how to handle other people, it's time to get back to you. The next chapter is like turning over a new leaf. We have dedicated enough time on overcoming problems, now it is time to start creating new, positive relationships based on everything you have learned about yourself so far.

7

How to Express Yourself and Build Genuine, Strong Friendships

Friends are necessary in our lives, there is no arguing this. Friends can play so many important roles. They can be the link to your childhood memories, and who you progressed into adulthood with. They are there to share the good, the bad, and the ugly, to laugh with until you cry, or to prop you up when you need a shoulder to cry on.

True friends will be able to put you in your place without making you take offense. They will also tell you when you need to stand up for yourself. Those who know you the best will be able to advise you on what's best for your life, but without leading your life for you.

Remember when you were in high school and you thought the friends you had would be with you for the rest of your life? Or when success was based on how large your social group was? This need to be liked often began at this very critical age.

But, as we grow up and change, so do our friendships. Different paths take us in different directions, or we simply grow apart, making way for new friends.

You might have closely examined your current friendships and learned that not everyone can be considered a real friend. Perhaps they didn't like that you have learned how to let go of the guilt and the need to please others, or worse, you have spotted people who are manipulating you for their own gain. Not to worry. Every new experience we have provides an opportunity to make new friends, and this time round, they will be friends who like you and respect you for who you are.

Learning to Proudly Express Who You Are

This is a great stage to have reached. Your new boundaries and goals to make you happy have inspired a new sense of motivation, and you are feeling more positive about life in general. This positivity is like a magnet, and it draws others to you. The 'new you' makes it easier to make new friends.

Before you can confidently meet new people, you need to look at ways you can express your new originality and perspective. It's great that you have discovered who you are, now let's work on furthering your individuality so that you aren't tempted to go back to pleasing others.

Expressing your originality goes beyond speaking your mind. And on that point, while it is great to express your opinions, be aware of becoming opinionated. You can't defend your political views if you don't know what you are defending. You can't talk about how difficult the Chinese language is if you have never tried to learn it. Never forget that while you have the right to your own opinion, others have a right to theirs as well. Not agreeing on something doesn't mean you won't have a long and fruitful friendship.

You will have had some unique experiences compared to

Stop People Pleasing

others, and now is a wonderful time to share these experiences. Even the situations that may have made you feel embarrassed, like social faux pas, have made you who you are today. Meeting new people is a chance for you to celebrate this.

I like to think of experiences like Lego bricks. Every new thing we try gets us a Lego brick. We watched a foreign film, tried a new supermarket, went skating, visited a new city—all these experiences earn us Lego bricks. Once you start putting your bricks together, your individuality begins to form. It's normal not to collect many Legos when we are younger because we tend to fit in with the crowd. As time goes on, and the more experiences you have, the more amazing things you can do with your Lego bricks.

Creating your own originality is also related to your appearance. How long have you spent wearing the clothes you thought were socially acceptable instead of going for the ripped jeans and boots you have dreamed of? Get the haircut you want, wear the clothes you feel comfortable in, and do it with pride and confidence. It's not important what others think about you, it's all about how you feel.

Let's look at a few more things to remember when expressing yourself with confidence:

- You will become an example that others follow. They will see how liberating it has been for you and start to feel more confident to do the same. All of a sudden, you will be a trendsetter!
- You have every right to express yourself as you see fit. You aren't hurting anyone. Your ideas and opinions may surprise some people. You may feel uncomfortable if

- someone doesn't agree with you, but nothing worse will happen.
- Some people might be shocked when you first start to express yourself. It is their job to get used to the new you.
- If you want to be heard, it's essential that you speak up. Don't let the moment to speak your mind pass and then feel resentful for not saying something.
- Remember it's okay not to get it perfectly right every time. Plenty of people find themselves in a situation where they can't express themselves. Center your mind and refocus on exactly what you want to say or do.
- Take one step at a time. Start small and as your confidence builds, you will be able to express yourself more confidently with groups, strangers, and other confident people.

How Can I Express My Passions When I Am Too Shy?

This is so difficult for many people. I had a client who was in her early 20s and loved to cross-stitch. She was incredibly patient and produced the most marvelous patterns, even from her own photos. But she was so shy she couldn't bring herself to show them to anyone. The first thing you can do is to display your passions in your home. We worked on framing some of her favorite cross-stitch patterns so that she could hang them on her walls. She didn't have to actively show her work, but it was the first thing that people noticed when they entered her home.

Social media can also be a great help here. You can take pictures of your various work and post them online. You don't have to make any comments or tell people that they are yours, just let others enjoy them.

As soon as you start receiving praise and compliments for your unique passions, you will become more confident in showing people.

The same theory can be said about the different types of clothes you want to wear. If you see a new outfit that is far from your normal style, but you absolutely love it, then buy it. Start off by wearing it around the house so that you can feel completely confident in it before going out in public. You can go to the supermarket first. Then you can wear it to a social event with friends and family. More often than not, we feel awkward about what we are wearing, and this draws attention to us, rather the outfit itself.

How Can I Share My Opinions Confidently?

The first thing to do is to be confident about your opinions. If you want to share your opinions about the political situation in Mexico, the first thing you need to do is check your facts to ensure you know what you are talking about. Jot down a few ideas and watch some videos of other people sharing their opinions on the same topic and pay attention to how they carry themselves.

Once you feel that you know all there is to know, bring the topic up with a friend and practice. Make a note of what parts of the conversation went well and which areas you can improve on, then take this to the drawing board for a bit more research if necessary.

Each time you practice, you can make the situation more challenging for yourself. So, the next time it could be with two or three friends, then the whole family, etc. As you stretch your comfort zones, you will become more confident talking about your opinions and your ideas.

How to Present Yourself Confidently in Public

Public speaking is our worst nightmare. It is the situation where we have to voice our ideas and opinions and hope that everyone likes them. We are so concerned about what everyone is going to think that our mind is overcome with anxiety and foreseeing a terrible outcome makes it impossible to focus on getting it right. Here are the most important things you can do to confidently express yourself when speaking in public:

Plan your outfit well

You really don't want to be sweating through your shirt or to have to bend down on stage while wearing a short skirt. These situations will add to the dread and fear. Wear something empowering, comfortable, and suitable.

Have bullet point notes of what you want to say

Don't have the whole text because you will end up reading a speech rather than giving a presentation. Having bullet point notes or ideas on flashcards keeps you focused on what you need to say, but it still provides you with freedom to improvise.

Change how you view your audience

They might be potential investors in your firm but focusing on this will only make you more nervous. While we don't suggest you imagine them all naked, you could imagine you are talking to a group of your old friends.

Choose one person to concentrate on during different parts of your presentation. Talking to a group of twenty is daunting, but if you focus on talking to each one individually, it takes the pressure off speaking to the entire group. Just make sure it isn't the same person all the time because this could make them feel uncomfortable.

Move around instead of sticking to one spot

Movement creates energy, and this will help engage your audience. Having a group of uninterested faces looking back at you will certainly not help your nerves.

Hold an item that you can use to distract yourself from the idea of being nervous

Any time I have to speak in public I always wear a ring. If the nerves are just too much, I use my thumb to twist it. It's not enough to distract the audience, but it does help me. Holding a pen can help too.

The great thing about talking in public is that each time you do it, it becomes easier, and you will feel a massive sense of achievement once it is finished, especially when people praise you for your efforts or, even better, ask for your expert opinion in follow-up questions.

Creating your own originality is an ongoing project. This is because each of your experiences will add to who you are. For this reason, it is ideal if you can try as many new things as possible. This is why going out and traveling by yourself is so vital. It pushes you and makes you do things that scare you.

◆

Write a Break-Up Letter to Your Old Self

If you are ready to truly embrace your own individuality that allows you to express yourself, a brilliant technique is to literally write a break-up letter to your old self. Mention the good times you have had, express your gratitude for all that you have learned, and explain why it is time to move on.

You might think this is a silly exercise, but you will appreciate an immense sense of liberation when you have finished the letter and signed it off from the new you. Be honest with your feelings, after all, nobody else is going to know about it, and even if they did, this shouldn't bother the new you.

How to Make Friends Without Feeling You Have to People Please

With the people you meet, you can now create equal relationships where you both can share how you feel. You don't need to agree with something because you don't want to lose the friendship, but because you know that it's perfectly okay for people to have their own opinions. You don't need to like the same things. The first stages are all about establishing your boundaries and respect. Here are some of the best ways to attract friends with kindness, but without the need to please people.

- Initiate conversations. It's a great sign of confidence and helps to overcome the first few minutes of shyness.
- Smile and take a genuine interest in what people are saying.
- Avoid potential controversial topics, like politics and religion, since there will be a time for this later on in the friendship.
- Ask original questions that remain within boundaries. Think about how you would feel if you were asked these questions, and if you would feel comfortable, then it's safe to say others will too. This is a great way to lead on to other new topics.
- Discover what you have in common. You may have traveled to different cities, but these cities share common ground. You might like different singers, but both performers appeared in the same concert.
- Concentrate on open body language, such as crossing your feet and not your legs, trying not to keep your hands behind your back, and making sure your eye contact is long enough but not too long.
- Don't make judgments about others, instead, find ways

you can compliment them and make them feel more comfortable.
- Be kind. Being kind means showing empathy for others, and by listening carefully to what they are saying, you will be able to relate to how they feel.
- Be the positive person. It is easy to focus on all of the negative aspects in the world today, but there are still numerous fantastic things that we can talk about. Be that person everyone wants to be around because of your optimism.
- Don't make comparisons between you and your new friends. They may have a degree and you don't, you might have wealthy parents and they don't, appreciate their uniqueness as much as you do your own.
- Make plans and stick to them. Suggest the next meeting, whether it's a coffee or a drink. Keep the activity quite tame until you learn more about each other's likes and dislikes.

When we are so eager to make friends, and more so with our recently found new identity, we can sometimes go a little overboard. Not in our individuality, but in trying too hard to impress. It's like we are conducting our own social experiment, and we can't wait to collect the results. We don't need to impress others; they will like us for who we are, or they won't. You will naturally impress them!

Finally, trust your new friendships. We have been hurt in the past, and we may be scolding ourselves for trusting those that we shouldn't have. But this is in the past, and there is little or nothing that we can do about this now. You can still protect yourself, but your new friends haven't done anything to cause you not to trust them, so it is only fair that you trust them.

How to Build a Strong Relationship that Will Last a Lifetime

The budding friendships are going well, and you have created the core foundations such as trust and respect. Now it's time to develop new habits that will lead to these friendships becoming much stronger so that they can handle any problems along the way.

For the most part, a strong relationship is about a lot of things we have already discussed, particularly your boundaries and what you are or aren't willing to do. You don't need to sit down with your new friend and have a "boundaries talk" because that might be a bit weird. However, you do need to be honest about your limits as things come up along the way. If your new friend doesn't realize you can't stand people fiddling with your car radio, they will never stop.

This all comes down to communication, or more specifically, effective communication. Most people think they are good at talking but forget the importance of listening. In fact, effective communication is about listening more than talking. Revise the 7 C's for effective communication, and make sure you can put a tick next to each.

Clear: What is the purpose or goal of your communication? If what you say is clear, people don't have to make assumptions.

Concise: Try to get to the point. There is no need to beat around the bush or repeat yourself several times.

Concrete: You have just the right amount of detail and facts to get the message across.

Correct: Obviously you want to make sure you are speaking correctly, but this also refers to adjusting your communication to suit the person. If you have a foreign friend, you might need to simplify the vocabulary or avoid complex expressions.

Coherent: Have you ever listened to someone who changes the subject faster than you can answer? It gets confusing! Try to keep your communication logical.

Courteous: Needless to say, we remain polite, but it also means not to be passive-aggressive or make subtle digs at people.

Complete: Your message must be complete and include all information as required by your audience.

The fastest way to see disturbances in a friendship is miscommunication. Something often small gets misinterpreted and then gets blown out of proportion. If you feel you have misunderstood anything, ask your friend straight away. Get it cleared up so that it doesn't ruin a great thing.

Let's look at a few more ways to fortify the friendship for the long run:

Agree to disagree

The best thing about having honest friendships is that you don't have to hide how you feel about something or your views. Rather than being a people pleaser and agreeing with everything, it is better that you and your friend simply agree to disagree on certain things.

Engage with them

We can probably all confess to doing this at least once in our lives in which people talk about something we aren't really interested in and our minds drift off. For a balanced friendship, it's important that you engage in your conversations. Ask questions to see if you can spark a bit of interest. People like it when they are acknowledged and are made to feel important, so it is a definite two-way street.

Make an effort to spend quality time together

The amount of time you spend together will depend on your other commitments and responsibilities. You should do some things together that you both enjoy and won't split your attention with another job or activity. At the same time, make sure you aren't spending all of your time together as you still need space.

Surprises and favors

Favors are a great way to offer someone support, and as long as you know that you can say no when you want to, doing someone a favor won't conflict with the new you. A surprise is a lovely way to show your friends that they matter. It doesn't have to be anything big, but if there is something they have been talking about for a while (a new book, tickets to a show, etc.), it can really show that you listen and you know them well.

Support each other

Not just through words but actions as well. Supporting your friends means you listen when they need you, and you offer a warm hug or a pat on the back when they need cheering up. It can also mean supporting their goals. If they want to branch into a new career or take up a different hobby, you are there for them.

Create new experiences together

Don't become reliant on your friends to do new things because you still have to try new experiences alone as part of your personal growth. But every once in a while, choose a random activity or a new place you can explore together. Better yet, create a list of things you want to try together and set a goal to complete them in a certain time.

Your friendships shouldn't have to be hard work. All of the above should come naturally or at least without a lot of effort. Not every friendship will be built to last the duration, and you don't want to force the matter because then the relationship isn't genuine. As long as you can keep the lines of communication open, you will be able to see the future of the friendship as strong or know when it is time to create some distance.

Overcoming Problems in a Friendship

As with any type of relationship, there will be problems along the way. It's not a sign that your friendship isn't meant to last, it just means it might need some extra work. Some changes in friendships will occur because of other relationships. We have all seen what happens when a friend starts a new relationship and tends to abandon others around them. There may also be changes in the dynamics of a group of friends.

Geography can take its toll. If a friend has to move to a new city or even a new part of town, it can disrupt the familiar routine you once had. New jobs have new demands, and we aren't as free as we want to be, or perhaps new hobbies lead to a change in interests.

None of the problems mentioned above are the fault of one person or the other, it's just a fact of life that circumstances change, and we have to adapt. Changes in our friendships can make us angry, jealous, or nervous. It's in times like these that we can't let our negative emotions destroy our relationships. Instead, talk to your friend about what is happening, discuss your feelings, listen to each other, and see if together you both can come up with solutions for the problems.

If things still feel a little raw or heated, take some time and space. This will allow you both the room you need to put things in perspective and see things from another point of view. It is a good idea to use your journal to express how you are feeling or to brainstorm some ideas.

Never blame the other person and don't accept them blaming you. Unless there is something obvious that one of you has done wrong, there is no point in playing the blame game as it only sparks negativity. If you have done something to upset the friendship, take responsibility for this and apologize. It might be all your friend needs to hear.

Your friendships will be some of the most important relationships in your life, and in many ways, it will be your friends who support you when you need help with your partner or family. All friendships should be built on trust, respect, and boundaries. Nobody should feel that they have to compromise who they are for a friendship, on the contrary, they should be encouraged to express their own originality.

Communication is fundamental at every stage and on every level of a friendship. Effective communication by listening and talking, expressing one's opinion and not hiding the truth from the very beginning will set the communicative expectations for the duration of the friendship. This is why it is crucial we get this right from the beginning.

We will now turn our attention back to ourselves, and instead of just friendships, let's learn how to become more assertive with people so that we can get what we want without causing offense or coming across as rude.

8
How to Stand Up for Yourself: 8 Assertiveness Techniques

Have you ever heard the expression, "There is a price to be paid for being nice."? For us people pleasers, the price can be very high. We can spend a significant part of our lives focusing on the needs of others rather than our own. Relationships tend not to reach their full potential because we are unable to truly express ourselves.

Being nice can cause turmoil when it has secondary effects. We can be nice to people because we don't want to hurt their feelings, even if they have hurt ours. In social settings, being nice means that our opinions or wishes are almost always never considered. In the work environment, being nice may stop us from confronting others about their negative behavior, and therefore the problem just becomes more apparent.

But we like being nice! It's who we are and an important part of what we believe in. Learning to say no to people doesn't mean we have to stop being nice. Our aim is to become more assertive so that we can put a stop to other people doing things we don't like or things that go against our values. It is about not allowing others to disrespect us and upset us. Being assertive lets us be good people, which still means we can be nice, but with boundaries.

How to Stand Up for Yourself: 8 Assertiveness Techniques

Assertive Does Not Imply Aggressive

It is not necessary to be aggressive to assert yourself. That being said, you will come across people who haven't learned the correct way to be assertive and the need to dominate is expressed in an aggressive way. Whether intentional or not, they become the bully in order to intimidate others into doing what they want. Being aggressive comes from the need to win. Being assertive is the need to find balance.

Our job is not to change these people. Instead, we are going to learn how to be assertive without feeling the need to be aggressive or to dominate others. We don't want to use our assertiveness to manipulate others into doing something for us, but to stand up for our beliefs, ideals, and for the things that make us happy in life.

How Will Being Assertive Benefit Me?

Since we are so worried about how others are going to feel, it is easy to forget the benefits of being assertive. Firstly, being assertive is a wonderful way to enhance communication. If done correctly, both parties are able to gain from the conversation without any feelings getting hurt in the process.

When problems are solved in a non-aggressive way, there is far less stress, and it prevents a negative atmosphere lingering around. This is particularly true in the work environment where issues have to be dealt with in the correct way so that it doesn't affect others in the workplace or the productivity of the team.

Being assertive ensures that others take you more seriously. It provides an opportunity for you to express your feelings genuinely without others resenting you for doing so. When a person knows they can count on your honesty, it is easier to build a trusting relationship, which is essential for your personal and professional life.

Though you might not feel completely confident when you first start to assert yourself, it still shows others that you are confident enough to stand up for what you believe is right. This encourages people to treat you as a confident person, which does wonders for actually building your confidence.

How to Become Assertive

Being assertive requires confidence and courage. This may not always come easily, so sometimes, it is worth turning the tables and seeing things from the other person's point of view. Let's say you have a friend who is never concerned about what you want to do on the weekends. He or she is a good friend but doesn't realize that they are affecting you. By being assertive in this situation, you are teaching them how to be a better friend by considering your feelings and ideas, in turn, strengthening the friendship.

Rather than experimenting to find the line between assertive and aggressive, it is better to learn how to become assertive with proven techniques.

Techniques to Become Assertive

1. Know exactly what you want

If you aren't sure of the purpose of your assertive conversation, then you are going to have a hard time getting a clear message across. Focus on just one thing rather than creating a list of items you want to discuss. If you don't like how someone touches you, this is what you want to change. If someone is demanding too much of your time, then your conversation is focused on this.

2. Speak in the first person and be careful of adverbs of frequency

Remember when we were learning how to deal with intrusive people and the importance of using the word "I"? The same is required when we want to be assertive. Using phrases like, "I don't feel respected in this situation," tells the other person exactly how you feel rather than generalizing. It also prevents you from starting a sentence with "you" followed by an insult, which will only fuel the situation.

Words like "always" and "never" should be avoided at all costs. Look at the difference between the sentences:

- I don't feel respected.
- You never respect me.

The first sentence clearly expresses your feelings whereas the second sentence has made it personal and encourages the other person to become defensive and the actual issue becomes buried in the emotions.

3. Remember what the issue is

This is another reason why using the correct vocabulary is so crucial. When we are assertive, we want the other person to be aware of how their behavior impacts us. It has no reflection on who they are as a person. Granted, they might not be the nicest person in the world, or they could be the love of your life. But this is not the issue, and our goal is to change the behavior, which is uncomfortable or upsetting as we know we aren't going to change the person.

When the focus of the conversation remains on the behavior and not the person, it is less likely to cause a defensive reaction, which again, becomes emotional and unproductive.

4. Remember the three C's of assertiveness

You are *confident* in your abilities to address the negative behavior. Your message is well-thought-out and *clear*. You communicate in a calm and *controlled* manner.

For all three to be present in your assertiveness, it is well worth preparing what you want to say in advance.

5. Focus on your verbal and non-verbal behavior

Aggressive verbal behavior is when we use phrases like, "That won't work," compared with assertive sentences such as, "I believe we could look at things in a different way." Being assertive means that you still listen and value what people are saying, but you can then ask open-ended questions because this will stimulate a conversation, rather than yes/no questions that will shut down the conversation.

Our non-verbal behavior should include an upright posture, eye contact, and a firm, clear voice. Not making eye contact or being too quiet points to a passive nature. On the other extreme, a loud person who insists on interrupting and staring at others is just being aggressive.

6. Don't waffle or beat around the bush

Your message should have three specific points:

- Explain the behavior that you are not happy with. Don't blame or judge.
- Explain how this makes you feel. Again, start your sentence with "I" and not "you." Tell the person exactly how you feel, so find the right words before you begin your conversation. This allows the other person to appreciate your true feelings and not just get a general idea.
- Explain the consequences of what they are asking. Maybe the result will be that you have to let someone else down or that you won't be able to fulfill your own responsibilities. They were probably so wrapped up in the issue that they didn't think of the potential consequences for others.

7. Give the other person a chance to speak

Sometimes all it takes is for you to clearly assert yourself for the other person to understand things from your point of view.

They might need a moment to process.

If you keep talking, you will never hear what their response is, and your assertiveness might be replaced with a long-winded complaint. The other person needs time to acknowledge their behavior before anything can be done about it. Ideally, from here, you can work together on finding the most appropriate solution.

8. Keep notes in your journal

Each time you assert yourself, you might get different responses or reactions. It is a good idea to keep a note of all of your experiences so that you can learn what worked for you and what didn't. It will highlight how well you are doing in some areas and other areas where you could improve your skills.

Becoming an expert in assertive behavior will take time and patience. Don't worry if you don't get it right the first time and don't be hard on yourself. Give yourself a confidence boost by looking back at those times you succeeded in being assertive and make a note of what you have learned.

How to Practice Being Assertive

It's perfectly normal that you want to practice how to be assertive before you actually have to confront the responses of someone. Often this is difficult until you are faced with a situation in which you are not happy, or you feel like your boundaries have been crossed.

Many people find it very useful to create scenarios where you can practice what you would say in each situation. This helps you to get faster at knowing what to say and provide you with more confidence when the time actually comes.

Let's look at some situations where being assertive is necessary along with what would be considered passive and aggressive. In each circumstance, think about defining the behavior you didn't like, how it made you feel, and the result of the other person's action. Play the conversation out in your mind or even in front of a mirror to get a better understanding of your body language.

What would you do if someone cuts in front of you in a queue?

- **Passive:** Do nothing, perhaps roll your eyes.
- **Aggressive:** Cause a scene in the store so that everyone saw their mistake.
- **Assertive:** Let the person know that you were next in the line and suggest they go to the back of the queue.

What would you do if a colleague makes a racist or sexist joke?

- **Passive:** Blush, lower your eye contact, and giggle a little so as not to feel left out.
- **Aggressive:** Call them out as a racist or sexist person and complain to management.
- **Assertive:** Remind them that that type of humor is inappropriate and repeat a clean yet funny joke.

What would you do if your friend, once again, turned up late?

- **Passive:** Tell them it's no problem, and it wasn't that long really.
- **Aggressive:** Leave without telling them you have gone.
- **Assertive:** Remind them that you are busy and ask if there was an important reason why they couldn't be on time.

What would you do if a relative continues to insult you?

- **Passive:** Avoid all family occasions where they could be.
- **Aggressive:** Insult them back.
- **Assertive:** Highlight how rude the insults are.

What would you do if a waiter brings you the wrong food?

- **Passive:** Eat it anyway. You believe it was an honest mistake, and they are very busy after all.
- **Aggressive:** Leave negative online reviews about the terrible service.
- **Assertive:** Explain that this isn't what you ordered and politely ask for them to bring you the right meal.

It is amazing how many real-life situations you can identify where others needed to be more assertive but went the wrong way about it. Even scenes on TV can leave you thinking about how things could have been handled better. Take inspiration from other people's experiences and use them to practice your new assertiveness techniques.

Being assertive requires a few core skills. You need to choose your words wisely, and never make the conversation about the person but rather on the behavior. You need to remain calm yet firm, stand tall, and maintain eye contact, without feeling the need to raise your voice.

If for any reason the other person becomes angry, insulting, or aggressive, you know that it is time to explain that you aren't making progress, and you will address the matter again at another time, then walk away. There is no point in continuing because the person will not be able to comprehend your point of view when they are hot-headed. Give them space to calm down but have the courage to come back when the time is right.

Ideally, at this point, you do not fear being assertive, but instead, welcome the chance to use your skills. Like with so many things in life, it is important to be prepared and know what you want to say, and practice is the best way to get better. If at any point you feel that it isn't going as you had planned, then go back to tactics like, "I will get back to you," as this will give you time to regroup and get your thoughts together. It is much better to take some time to think about how you can deal with the situation in a different way than it is to back down.

When done correctly, nobody looks at an assertive person and sees them as rude. They see a person who is brave enough to stand up for what they believe in and what matters to them. People will respect you for this, and they will like you, so never feel guilty for being assertive.

9

Troubleshooting Guide: What if Nothing Seems to Be Working?

We are coming close to the end of this book, and you have learned some of the most effective ways to say no without offending others. You are probably already seeing some of the benefits at work, even if you haven't been able to put everything into practice yet.

It is also possible that you aren't seeing the results you had expected or any results yet. This doesn't mean that you won't get there. It simply means that you are still working through the process.

Some people have a learning curve that is more up and down than a Ferris wheel. You might have a week or two of seeing massive improvements in your life, but then months of nothing. This can be hard because it tugs at your motivation to keep going.

If you are having problems with seeing the results, it might help to remember just how long the word no has been a problem for you. It begins as toddlers. For a lot of young ones, their first word is no because it's a word they hear so often. They go to touch the cooker: "No." They put something in their mouth: "No." Yet then, when the children say no, their parents feel the need to punish them. When a child says no to going to bed, they are testing their boundaries, but they are still reprimanded for doing so.

Our parents' warnings continue while we are teenagers, warning us to say no to peer pressure. But the signals are now mixed as to be polite, and we must say yes and be willing to help others. It will be a long time before no isn't considered rude in social situations.

The point is whether you have had 20, 30, or 50 years of life experience, the words yes and no have had a significant impact on the person you have become, and it will take time to change this behavior. Before you start to panic that nothing is going to work, remember to have a little patience and to stop being so hard on yourself.

Troubleshooting #1. Not Appreciating the Extent Of the Problem

It may be possible that while you nod your head as you are reading the words, you still haven't acknowledged the extent of your people pleasing problem. You still firmly believe that you are being nice and want the best for others. A close look at the harsh reality of the situation could be what you need to get the progress under way.

- It won't help your relationships in the long run. In the end, the strain you put on yourself to please others will make others take advantage of you, and the relationships will weaken.

- Your anxiety in situations where you want to say no but can't will get worse because you are moving further away from your goal.
- You will become more stressed as you won't have any time for yourself.
- Mentally and physically, you will become drained, and this will have an impact on your diet, your sex life, your sleep, and your mood.
- You run the risk of burnout, relationships ending, and depression.

This exercise isn't designed to scare you. More than anything, it should be used as a reminder that people pleasing doesn't just go away, unfortunately, it may just escalate.

Troubleshooting #2. Unclear Goals

Speaking to clients who are in the same situation, the problem can be that the person hasn't focused on their goals enough and what they actually want to change. The goals might be too general, and they haven't been broken down into achievable steps. The goal, "I want to be happy," is a good start, but ultimately, it's the same goal we all have and not personal to you. Let's look at how we can restructure our goals.

The ultimate goal is to be happy, but ask yourself what you need to get there.

- I want to advance my career.
- I want to improve my relationship with my partner.

- I want time to myself on the weekends.

Now that the goal has been broken down into three reasons to help you achieve happiness, you can further break them down into manageable steps that are easier to accomplish:

- I need to take some courses to improve certain skills.
- I need to get better at communicating how I feel.
- I need to manage my time in advance so that I don't overbook my schedule.

Goals are essential for every aspect of our lives. Without them, we fall into the habit of getting up, going through the motions, and going to sleep. There is nothing to make us want to be better and nothing to strive for. If you feel like you haven't planned your goals properly, go back to this stage, and create both long-term and short-term goals.

Most importantly, remember to update your goals. Perhaps you have read this book in a week or a few months, and the chances are that some things are now different, or you have achieved some of your short-term goals. Take time to reassess your goals once a month.

Troubleshooting #3. Your First No Was a Terrible Experience

This has happened to the best of us. You have done everything you should have to prepare for the situation, and you honestly felt like you did everything right, but the person expressed every emotion in the book. You were laughed at, shouted at, and you just felt humiliated. This has resulted in you never wanting to go through the same experience again and made you realize that it is just easier to keep saying yes.

The first thing to remember is that the reaction of this person is not your fault, and you should not feel embarrassed or upset for the way they treated you. This is on them and only them. Although there is no excuse for their behavior, and you shouldn't let them get away with it, you can only assume they were having another personal problem that caused them to fly off the handle.

Try to turn your pain into frustration. Allow yourself to be angry at how you were treated because nobody has the right to treat another human being that way. Then find an outlet for your anger so that you are emotionally ready to look for a solution. You may not like it, but you are going to have to address this person again using your new assertive techniques.

More often than not, when the person is confronted about their behavior and you provide them with a chance to respond, they will see the error of their ways, and you will both come to an agreement.

Troubleshooting #4. You Can't Find the Right Words

After so long of not expressing how you feel, it can be difficult to find the words to describe exactly how you feel and then hope that the other person can understand where you are coming from.

People pleasing is a sign of poor emotional intelligence, the inability to understand, use, and manage your own emotions.

We run from confrontation instead of standing up for ourselves and what we feel is right. Expanding your emotional vocabulary can help improve your emotional intelligence, allowing you to better understand your feelings.

Whether you are letting others know your new boundaries or asserting yourself, it makes sense to find the words before you start a conversation. For example, the word sad is not going to do the job because it can mean so many different things to different people. You can be sad because of the weather, or because you broke a nail, or your football team lost. You can be sad when you feel insulted, embarrassed, or ridiculed.

Try using an online thesaurus to expand your vocabulary. Type in the word you feel and see if there are words that better describe your emotion.

Sad: downhearted, out of sorts, regretful, heartbroken, pitiful, mournful, etc.

Out of sorts implies you are sad but because of something that isn't normal, mournful suggests you have lost something, regretful because you have made a mistake, or broken-hearted because of a fight with a loved one. Each word gives the other person a clearer idea than "sad" would. In times when you can't seem to put your finger on how you are feeling, look for similar words while you are preparing what you want to say.

Troubleshooting #5. Nobody is Accepting Your No

That's okay! This is nothing you have done wrong, but it's just that people aren't used to you saying no, which may require another go. The good news is now that you have already said no, it will be easier the next time round, even if you ended up saying yes the last time.

When the moment arises for you to say no to someone who has not accepted your answer the first time, you need to start off by reminding them that you have already had this conversation, and something simple like, "I have already said no because I am unavailable," will do. Then draw their attention away from the original plan or idea with an alternative option like arranging a plan for a different night or reorganizing the workload so that all individuals are happy.

If people continue to ignore your no, then it is time to become more assertive without crossing the boundary and becoming aggressive. This could be something as simple as adjusting your body language or speaking more firmly. Don't be scared to remind them again that you have said no and that you don't appreciate feeling pressured into doing something. Again, say that you are open to other ideas. If this doesn't work, walk away, but don't back down when the conversation comes up again. Instead of being upset or frustrated, see it as a friendly game of the battle of the wills.

Troubleshooting #6. The Word No Just Won't Come Out

Because of the fear and guilt that we associate with no, some people get themselves so worked up about saying no that it becomes impossible, as if you have put too much pressure on them to do it.

Troubleshooting Guide: What if Nothing Seems to Be Working?

In times like this, we choose words and phrases that imply no without us having to actually say the word. Phrases like, "Thank you for the invitation, but I can't," will have the same result yet takes away the pressure of saying no.

More often than not, when you start to see the results with the phrases that mean no, you will start to feel confident enough to decline. You get to experience the benefits, like freeing up your time and not having to work overtime, when you don't want to without the turbulent sensation of saying no.

Overcoming your people pleasing disorder is a steep learning curve, but remember that it is a curve that is going up and not down. Things will only get better when you know exactly what you want to achieve and keep practicing.

We keep talking about the importance of patience and taking time to work through the process, but there are also situations in which you need to see results far quicker. For this, we will finish off with a plan for those who want to see results in just two weeks.

10

Taking Action to Stop People Pleasing in Two Weeks

It is advisable to take the necessary time you need for each step, whether that's a month or a year. This gives you the time to perfect each stage and learn how to handle each situation as you want to.

On the other hand, if there is an occasion coming up, or you need to see the results faster, the following guide will allow you to speed things up and see results from day one. The goal is to be able to confidently say no in two weeks. You might want to take some of the techniques from the following list to use them in conjunction with other methods you have learned from the previous chapters.

Really, the action plan is a recap of what we have discovered so far that can be used when time is of the essence. The most important thing is that you are comfortable and confident when you practice your steps.

Day 1: Preparation

This is a day dedicated to mentally preparing yourself for saying no. You look at who you are now and decide on the core aspects you want to change. It won't be as extensive as the self-discovery journey in chapter two because that might be too much in a short period of time, but you can list four things you want to change and four new goals to work toward.

Buy a journal today so that you can start keeping track of your emotions and make a note of what is working for you and what you might want to leave to try for another time.

Day 2: Taking Care of Yourself

Create a mantra or write down simple sentences like, "I will not feel guilty for putting my needs first," "I do deserve to be happy," or, "I am a kind, good person." Remind yourself that only you can control your feelings and actions, and that you are not responsible for other people. Fill yourself with positive thinking, self-love, and self-worth. Learn what you need to be emotionally and physically well. Set out a new schedule that allocates time for you. It will depend on your current responsibilities, but I would recommend fifteen minutes a day for exercise, meditation, or exploring things that you want to create new experiences.

Make one change that speaks to your originality and who you are. Let others see the new you, even if you aren't saying no yet. A new outfit or haircut can be a great start to show others you are breaking away from the old you.

Day 3: Deciding What You Should Say Yes and No To

From the minute you wake up to the moment you go to sleep, analyze every situation that requires a yes or no answer. Decide on how the situation makes you feel and based on these feelings, you can decide on whether you will say yes or no going forward.

If you examine all yes/no situations, you will realize that there are so many in just one day. Some of them you will feel you want to say yes to, others are a definite no, and some need more time. This is the fastest way to learn what your boundaries are, but you may want to keep your journal close by so you can reflect on your feelings that evening.

Day 4: Stop Saying Yes

It is a lot to ask to jump into the no on day four (however if you feel prepared and confident, you can). Today is about not saying yes if you don't want to. From day three, you now know what you are willing to say yes to because in saying yes, you will be happy. Say yes to only the things that are within your boundaries and will make you content. If you are unsure, let the person know that you will get back to them.

Day 5: Providing Alternatives

On this day, you practice offering an alternative to something you don't want to do. You could use phrases like, "What about if we did XYZ instead." You aren't saying yes, but technically you're not saying no either. The hope is that the other person understands you don't want to do something, but you would rather think of an alternative plan, and therefore they aren't offended.

Day 6: The "Sandwich Technique"

You may have heard of this as the "Build Break Build technique" for providing constructive criticism, but it can also work for saying no, and it's another way to assert yourself without mentioning the actual word.

Start by highlighting something you are happy about, follow up with something you aren't satisfied with, and finish off with a positive solution. Imagine your boss wants you to finish your part of the project as well as someone else's who is off sick:

"I am grateful you have thought of me to do this, and while I love the opportunity, I am concerned I won't be able to complete both deadlines on time. Is it possible if I ask the assistant to handle my phone calls today so that I can dedicate myself to this project?"

You have sandwiched your no between a thank you and a solution, which is a perfect solution for both parties to gain.

Day 7: Reassess and Celebrate

It's been a full-on week that will have brought about some very positive changes. You have learned a lot about yourself, and you will have been able to practice the foundations of saying no. You may have felt some resistance, but nothing that has upset you or caused you to back down from your goal. Today is about taking some time to do something you want to do as a reward for your hard work. Take some time out to assess how you are feeling and prepare yourself for the next week.

Day 8: Freeing Yourself From the Need for Approval

As the days go by, we will start to crank things up, and this begins with creating a harder outer skin. Today is about being aware of how people feel but not turning it back on to you. When you say no and someone is shocked, this doesn't mean you have done anything wrong. It is a day to remember that you don't need anyone's approval to do what is best for you or what makes you happy. By letting go of the need for approval, you can focus on what you truly want, knowing that some will like you for who you are and others won't.

Day 9: Finding Your Anger and Stress Outlets

You might have encountered a few difficult people by now, and their persistence has frustrated you. You will probably find it hard to stop replaying your conversation with them in your mind and trying to see what you could have done differently.

You may need to take today to find out how to get rid of the anger, stress, and/or anxiety before you face this person again. Try shouting, screaming, punching a pillow, swimming, dancing, singing, painting, or writing in your journal. Try any activity that calms you down and allows you to go back to thinking about the solution without emotions getting in the way.

Day 10: Adjust the Balance in Your Relationships

In just ten days, you will start to feel that you are more confident in expressing how you really feel. Without creating a big dramatic scene, talk to your loved ones about the changes you want to make in your life and explain what you now feel comfortable doing. Remind them that you love them and want your relationships to be even stronger, but for this, you need to start putting yourself first.

Day 11: Saying No Without the Need to Justify

On day eleven, we keep it short and simple. We are polite in our no, we thank the person for the invitation or offer, then explain that we are unavailable. If this leads the person to question you further or cross the line by asking you why not, you can apologize and say you don't feel comfortable having to explain yourself. Ensure your body language is neither passive nor aggressive and feel proud of successfully asserting yourself.

Day 12: The "Broken Record Technique"

Today is a way to further your assertiveness by using the "Broken Record Technique." It literally is as it sounds, and you keep repeating your sentence like a broken record on a turntable. If a person asks you to do something you are not happy about doing, you respond by saying something like, "No, thank you, I have plans." They might rephrase the same request and hope for a different answer, but you stick to the same response. They are likely to persist, but so will you.

This technique allows you to easily stand your ground without being tempted to offer explanations. It doesn't require a high degree of self-control and determination, which is why it wasn't mentioned in the chapter related to asserting yourself. Nevertheless, if you feel confident that you can stick to it, this technique is one of the most effective methods for assertiveness.

Day 13: The Big No

Up until now, you may have been practicing the no word on people you feel more confident with. At this stage, it is time to tackle the one that perhaps you have been dreading. You have had plenty of good experiences over the last two weeks and it is time to put it all into practice. Remember the necessity to prepare beforehand and make sure that you are clear and confident about what you want to say.

Day 14: You Have Done It

Day fourteen should be a day when you have no plans or commitments. You have worked so hard and accomplished massive amounts in a short period of time. Today you can tick off some goals, stay in your pajamas, or make plans with people if you want to. You can take a walk in the park and appreciate a sense of relief and a new way of living your life. Today you can explore the benefits of meditation and mindfulness. It is

Taking Action to Stop People Pleasing in Two Weeks

a day to completely soak up what it feels like not to live in fear and anxiety. Today is the day to feel yourself in your new state, appreciate who you have become, and plan where you want to go next.

This day allows you to get in touch with the emotions you have felt over the last thirteen days and to really understand the changes you have made within yourself. You can then create a plan for the next two weeks, two months, or two years, and you can do so knowing that the focus of your goals will be what you need and what you deserve.

The two-week action plan for successfully saying no isn't set in stone. Feel free to adapt it to your needs. You might feel it is more suitable to address your relationships earlier on, or you may want to use the sandwich/broken record technique from day one. Sometimes the situations mentioned don't come up in the fourteen days that you have dedicated to this plan. You can still take the fourteen days to prepare for the moment that you do need it and keep practicing scenarios in your mind in the meantime. Follow your heart and your instincts, and use the techniques as you see fit. Everyone is unique!

Conclusion

Congratulations! You are now fully aware of your people pleasing disorder. Not only are you determined to make your life a happier one where you are in control, but you are learning how to overcome the guilt of saying no because you have realized you can no longer satisfy everyone's needs and your own.

What an exhilarating journey, and it's only just beginning. What you have learned in this book will help you for the rest of your life. You don't just close the book on this chapter, so to speak, because the learning and effort is continuous. But you will notice that as you grow as a person, and your life situations change, saying no to people pleasing will become a part of your daily routine, a habit just like getting dressed or driving to work. You won't notice the effort, and it will come naturally.

At this point, many people ask me what the ultimate technique is for saying no. Although vague, I often say it depends on the day. You may have noticed by now that some methods seem to work well on one day, and not so much the following. Overcoming people pleasing is a complex task that will not be the same for every individual. Some people are more determined while others take a little longer to shift those feelings of guilt.

Having goals made such a difference for me, as it does for practically all of the clients I work with. As well as working toward something and remaining focused, having goals helps motivate you after any type of setback. If you do have a difficult time saying no to someone, you can go back and look at your goals to remind yourself why you are working so hard to make these changes.

I spent a long time learning how to communicate with others. Far too many people think that it is just talking. I worked hard on my verbal and non-verbal communication, and in particular, the words and phrases I wanted to use. I strongly recommend working on this. One of my clients noticed a huge difference in how people responded to him just by standing up straighter and making more eye contact. Another learned very quickly the power of changing "you" to "I" and removing all the blame from a conversation to prevent things from becoming emotional.

When asking clients what technique they found the most beneficial, the larger percentage of people had said the ability to say no without actually having to say the word. Phrases like, "I would love to, but I already have plans," doesn't put pressure on you to flatly turn someone down but, in most cases, it still has the desired result. You free up some of your time so that you can put some of your needs first. Even if you don't master saying no in all situations straight away, this allows people to start taking back some of the control over their lives and let go of some of the anxiety. It also gives them a taste of the benefits, and it inspires them to keep trying other techniques.

There are other times when the best solution is just to politely say no. No fuss, no drama, just a "No, thank you."

To decide which technique to use will very much depend on your feelings at the time, which is why it is crucial to listen to them and what they are trying to tell you. Experimenting with the different techniques in this book will allow you to determine which work better for you in various situations. You are building your confidence and empowering yourself to be ready for any type of no.

The journal is an outstanding tool for everyone. It allows you to start expressing how you feel without fear of other people mocking or rejecting your emotions. It provides a space for you to plan and set goals, and a place for you to follow your progress. When a client said they wished they could carry their journal with them everywhere, the idea came for the pocket list.

On a piece of A5 paper, copy the following ten pointers. Do it by hand since the extra effort helps the message sink in and become more meaningful than typing and printing.

1. Learn who you are and find your originality.
2. Know what you need to make you happy, what to say yes to, and what to say no to.
3. Choose two or three phrases that imply no without having to say it.
4. Every day learn a new word for how you are feeling and imagine how you would assert yourself in a situation you have seen before.
5. Calm down, breathe, and find an outlet for your emotions.
6. Keep your messages firm, clear, to the point, and confident.

Conclusion

7. Remember the Sandwich or Broken Record Technique.
8. Stay away from manipulators.
9. Tell yourself you deserve this and that you are a wonderful person.

On the back of the piece of paper, write your mantra at the top of the page and then three short-term goals and three long-term goals. Now fold the paper up and take it everywhere you go. Any time you feel like you are losing your focus, or you need to bring your mind back to saying no, you can review your piece of paper.

You should be feeling proud of yourself. Deciding that you are going to be happy and that you will be absolutely fine regardless of whether people like you or not can be a scary process. You have made a decision that is going to change your life, not just for the better, but for the best, and you don't have to sacrifice anything in return. Rather, your relationships will be more meaningful, you will have time to enjoy life, and you will become emotionally stronger.

All you need to do now is keep going. Take the tools you have learned from this book and take one day at a time. Understand that there might be moments when you find it difficult, or you don't get the reaction you want, but you will still learn from this and you can keep working toward your dreams. From this moment, you no longer have to feel the need to apologize or explain yourself, to allow people to pester or even manipulate you until you say yes. No one can deter you from your personal growth.

If you have enjoyed this book, I would be very grateful if you could leave your review on Amazon so that I can continue my learning curve. I am glad that I have been able to take this journey with you, and I am positive that this is the beginning of amazing things for you.

References

Alpert, J. (2020, February 6). 7 Tips for saying no effectively. Retrieved from https://www.inc.com/jonathan-alpert/7-ways-to-say-no-to-someone-and-not-feel-bad-about-it.html

Canter, L. (2019, June 3). The dangers of being a people-pleaser. Retrieved from https://medicalxpress.com/news/2019-06-dangers-people-pleaser.html

Heger, E. (2020, June 22). 7 benefits of meditation, and how it can affect your brain. Retrieved from https://www.insider.com/benefits-of-meditation

HuffPost is now a part of Verizon Media. (n.d.). Retrieved from https://www.huffpost.com/entry/whos-business-are-you-in_b_7207938

Hughes, L. (2017, March 2). How to stop feeling anxious right now. Retrieved from https://www.webmd.com/mental-health/features/ways-to-reduce-anxiety

Ideas, I. (2014, December 10). Break your bad habits: Letting go of defence mechanisms. Retrieved from http://www.infideas.com/break-bad-habits/

Jong, K. (2019, December 19). The art of being yourself: 5 ways to embrace authenticity as your way of life. Retrieved from https://katiedejong.com/authentically-you/

Smith, A. (2019, December 17). 6 Steps to discover your true self. Retrieved from https://www.success.com/6-steps-to-discover-your-true-self/

Snape, H. (2019, August 27). Overcoming fear of rejection. Retrieved from https://www.helensnape.com/peoplepleaserblog/2019/8/27/overcoming-fear-of-rejection

Tartakovsky, M. (2018, July 8). 7 Tips for setting boundaries at work. Retrieved from https://psychcentral.com/blog/7-tips-for-setting-boundaries-at-work/

The Broken-record response in communication. (n.d.). Retrieved from https://www.thoughtco.com/broken-record-response-conversation-1689041

The seven Cs of communication—Edexec.co.uk. (n.d.). Retrieved from https://edexec.co.uk/the-seven-cs-of-communication/

https://positivepsychologyprogram.com/self-confidence-self-belief/

https://www.mindtools.com/selfconf.html

https://www.theladders.com/career-advice/the-8-most-effective-ways-to-get-back-on-track-after-you-messed-up-and-finally-stay-there

YourCoach Gent. (2019) S.M.A.R.T. goal setting | SMART | Coaching tools | Yourcoach.be. Retrieved 24 April 2019, from https://www.yourcoach.be/en/coaching-tools/smart-goal-setting.php

Michl, L. C., McLaughlin, K. A., Shepherd, K., & Nolen-Hoeksema, S. (2013). Rumination as a mechanism linking stressful life events to symptoms of depression and anxiety: Longitudinal evidence in early adolescents and adults. Retrieved from https://www.ncbi.nlm.nih.gov/pmc/articles/PMC4116082/

Psychologist World. (n.d.) Psychology of choice. Retrieved from https://www.psychologistworld.com/cognitive/choice-theory#references